Joan Samuelson's *Running* *for* WOMEN

Joan Samuelson's
Running for WOMEN

By Joan Benoit Samuelson
and Gloria Averbuch

Rodale Press, Inc.
Emmaus, Pennsylvania

Cover and Book Designer: Charles Beasley
Cover Photographer: David Madison/Duomo

Library of Congress Cataloging-in-Publication Data

Samuelson, Joan Benoit.
    [Running for Women]
    Joan Samuelson's running for women / by Joan Benoit
Samuelson and Gloria Averbuch.
        p.   cm.
    Includes index.
    ISBN 0–87596–239–4 paperback
    1. Running for women.   2. Physical fitness for women.
I. Averbuch, Gloria, 1951–   . II. Title.   III. Title: Running
for women.
GV1061.18.W66S26   1995
796.42'082—dc20   94–44238

Distributed in the book trade by St. Martin's Press

2 4 6 8 10 9 7 5 3 1 paperback

NOTICE

This book is intended as a reference volume only. The information given here is designed to help you make informed decisions about your exercise and fitness program. It is not intended as a substitute for any professional medical or fitness advice. As with all exercise programs, you should seek your doctor's approval before you begin.

Photography Credits

To my mother and father, Nancy and Andre Benoit,
for whom my cheers will never end.
—J.S.

In memory of Ann Ohlstein (1936–1993) and to my daughters,
Yael and Shira.
—G.A.

In memory of Fred Lebow and George Sheehan,
both of whom perfected the art of running as a metaphor for life.
—J.S. and G.A.

CONTENTS

PART II
RUNNING FASTER AND STRONGER

PART III
THE WINNING EDGE

The third of four children, Joan is pictured here with her three brothers, Andre, Jr., Peter and John (*seated*), and mother, Nancy.

While she was coached by John Babington, Joan represented the Liberty Athletic Club. She is shown here competing in the Bonne Bell 10-K in 1978.

Near her home in Freeport, Joan contemplates the natural beauty of the Maine coast.

PREFACE

I have been running competitively and with a deep passion for over 20 years; that period has included high school competition, national and international competition, an Olympic gold medal and a continuing quest to reach new goals.

Over the years much has changed in my life, but my focus on running has remained consistently strong. It is with a sense of great joy and inner drive that I have maintained my running on every level from the day-to-day training to the remarkable events like the Olympic Games.

Running has been a major part of my life. It has been a series of setting goals and striving to achieve those goals. Like so many women, sometimes my needs and interests are congruous, and sometimes they compete with each other for my time, energy and focus. Running has provided me with countless challenges and rewards as has my marriage and the birth of my children. But of all

In 1977, Joan (*far right*) competed in some track meets for Boston College. Next to her is Lynn Jennings.

As a senior at Bowdoin College, Joan was cross-country champion and all-American.

the challenges I have faced, the greatest one has been the quest for combining my family and career.

Continually setting goals and striving to achieve them is what makes life worthwhile. My first book, *Running Tide*, ends with the attainment of a personal dream: an Olympic gold medal. But that was not the end of the road. I went on to establish a new American record in the marathon and to set my sights on a sub-2:20 marathon—a goal that still sustains and motivates me. And whether or not I achieve that sub-2:20, I'd like to be part of the competition when it happens.

That's the professional aspect of where life took me after my first book. While winning a gold medal was truly all the wonderful clichés one imagines, since that time, I have been fortunate to have other life-altering experiences.

Having my children has been an even greater highlight than my athletic career. The first time I took my newborn daughter out, I

The thrill of winning Boston the second time in 1983. Joan's outstanding course record was a world record as well: 2:22:43.

stopped at the local market and bought a lottery ticket—the first and only time I have ever done that. I reasoned that I might as well try my luck at everything. I just felt like I was the luckiest person in the world.

It is good fortune—both professionally and personally—that has been the key to my ultimate happiness. I think one of the most important changes in my life since having children is that I feel I have attained a greater sense of inner peace. Before having children I was mainly focused on one thing: my running. As an athlete I had no tolerance for excuses when things didn't go well for me. Now I am more patient with myself. After all, I have a wider perspective.

Children keep you honest. They make you realize what your priorities really are or at least what they ought to be. Once the stopwatch was important for checking splits or a training pace; now I check my watch to pick up the children at school or to meet the babysitter. Competition—running times and finishing place—have

Winning the Olympic trials marathon only 17 days after arthroscopic knee surgery took real commitment and gritty determination. Joan's victory was considered an amazing feat. Afterward, she collapses against a railing in pain and relief.

no meaning to my children, so, by association, those things have changed their meaning for me as well. But I still desire to push myself, to have a focus outside my family, because for me they go hand in hand. Doing something for yourself like running, and using it to test yourself, will only make you feel better about your career or your family role.

If running overshadows my parenting or my parenting prevents me from doing that something for myself outside the family, I think both roles are shortchanged. What's more, if I feel good about my relationship with my husband and the children, then even a minor breakthrough in running seems so much sweeter.

The challenge and the energy running requires may be a selfish pursuit, but it actually motivates me to be stronger in my relationships. Being an athlete helps me to know I will give that extra effort when it comes to caring for another's needs. When things don't go well in a race, it's easy to say, "It's not my day," but the race at

Three months after the Olympic trials came Joan's golden victory in Los Angeles. Her joy is shared with family as she hugs her mother afterward.

home never ends. Maybe this is the reason I've never dropped out of a race—either the one on the road or at home!

For most of my running career the greatest challenge has been getting the most from myself without going over the edge: getting sick or injured. In fact, I suppose what I am best known for as a runner is my drive, unpredictability and the ability to perform well against the odds. This is best illustrated by my well-publicized comeback when I won the 1984 Olympic trials marathon only 17 days after arthroscopic knee surgery.

Much of this book is about learning to reach for the stars while at the same time understanding our limits. There have been times that my drive has gone out of control. There have been times when my go-for-it approach backfired. I broke down or was injured. Although my body could not always withstand my efforts, determination and an iron will have helped me reach my limits. That lesson is much of the basis for the theme of this book: balance.

In Chicago in 1985, Joan set an American record for the marathon, 2:21:21, which still stands today.

There is an art to maintaining that careful blend of physical and mental effort.

After the Los Angeles Olympics and after marrying and having children, the demands in my life radically changed—both professionally and personally. Now I feel a great understanding and empathy for women who seek to live active, full lives—without becoming overwhelmed. And this is why I feel strongly about sharing my knowledge with other women runners from those at the top of the competitive ranks to those just taking their first steps.

This book is about running and, to me, running is about balance and wholeness, about the yin and yang of both work and play. Training may be hard work but it has always been enjoyable for me. Even while I am working hard, I'm having fun. There's a Maine ethic that says, "In order to play, you have to work." I like to use the example of the seasons. In winter, you have to shovel snow in order

Joan with her family today: husband, Scott, daughter, Abby, and son, Anders.

to build snow people. In spring, you have to dig and plant the garden in order to welcome the flowers or vegetables. In summer, you have to haul big buckets of wet sand in order to build sand castles. In fall, you have to rake the New England leaves in order to make a pile to jump into. As a child these seasonal activities were extremely important to me. They built the foundation of character and perseverance that I have called upon time and time again as an athlete and as a person.

It is my sincere hope that this book will help you to develop strength and wisdom as a runner and that your running will reside harmoniously with all other aspects of your life. As every runner knows, running is about more than just putting one foot in front of the other; it is about our lifestyle and who we are.

—*Joan Samuelson*

ACKNOWLEDGMENTS

This book would never have been started or completed if it had not been for the help, encouragement, coaching and support of many people. As I said after my win in the 1984 Olympic Marathon, I owe my thanks to the many people who have supported me through the good and the bad, the ups and the downs. I feel compelled to extend those same heartfelt thanks to those who helped me with this marathon of book writing. It is no coincidence that many of those I thank now were included among those I thanked after finishing my race in the Los Angeles Coliseum.

First and foremost, I owe much gratitude to my collaborator—and, as a result of working on this book together for countless hours, my new good friend—Gloria Averbuch. I am truly indebted to Gloria for her patience, dedication and ability to sort through my many training and racing stories while keeping me on pace with the project. Gloria's suggestions and feedback were most valuable when it came to deciding what information to include in each chapter and subject area. Her insight into our sport served to broaden the areas we chose to include in the book.

Our thanks also go to Paul Friedman, two-time Olympic trials marathon qualifier, for his support during the writing of this book. His technical assistance in the formulation of our training charts and his honest feedback from the beginning to the end of the project helped us to provide the best and most recent information possible.

My sincere thanks must also be extended to John Babington, assistant coach for the U.S. women's track team for the 1996 Olympics, who worked with Paul and me to create the training charts and who contributed the drills. John was also a dedicated and diligent contributor of valuable information throughout other parts of the book. His experience and expertise as a longtime coach of the Liberty Athletic Club and of women runners of all abilities, from the internationally famous to beginners, is recognized and respected by coaches and athletes around the world.

A special heartfelt thanks to Deb Merrill, a certified neuromuscular therapist in private practice in Brunswick, Maine, for her thorough and intelligent work. With great dedication and enthusiasm, she contributed a substantial amount to the project. I've been working with Deb for several years. She has played an integral role in my running since the change in my biomechanics as a result of childbirth. Deb's work as a neuromuscular therapist is outstanding, and her advocacy of self-care is valuable to countless runners.

Thanks also to exercise physiologists Jack Daniels, Ph.D., of the State University of New York at Cortland, and Robert Vaughan, Ph.D., of Baylor University Medical Center in Dallas, who contributed their expertise to this book as well as to the evolution of women's running with their scientific research. Their countless studies and findings have been of great value and inspiration to coaches and athletes everywhere.

This book is cutting edge thanks to the research and contributions of noted nutrition author Nancy Clark, R.D., nutritional consultant at Sportsmedicine in Brookline, Massachusetts, sports psychologist Linda Bunker, Ph.D., of the University of Virginia in Charlottesville, Mona Shangold, M.D., noted author and sports medicine gynecologist at Hahnemann University Hospital in Philadelphia, Rosemary Agostini, M.D., of the Virginia Mason Medical Center in Seattle, and Ramona Melvin, personal trainer and fitness expert at Equinox Health Club in New York City. Experts in their respective fields, these women have gained the respect of women runners everywhere. Their contributions to our sport have enabled female athletes to excel and flourish in good health.

Warm thanks are extended to Judy Mahle Lutter, president of the Melpomene Institute for Women's Health Research in St. Paul—a wonderful resource of information on women's health issues. Judy provided us with her network of contacts, which resulted in working with several of our valuable contributors— second to none in their specialties.

A special thanks to Robert E. Leach, M.D., editor of the *American Journal of Sports Medicine*, for honing the details in describing and defining my running-related injuries. Dr. Leach's nurturing personality and his care for my well-being during my treatment has inspired me throughout my career to compete to the best of my ability and to give whatever I can back to the sport.

Tom Fleming deserves credit for his technical contributions in different areas of our book. Tom's involvement with the sport of running as an elite athlete, coach and owner of a specialty running store in Bloomfield, New Jersey, gave him the ability to refine the details of everything from shoes to training and racing.

Thanks also to Michael Sargent, M.D., team physician at the University of Vermont in Burlington, for his intelligent medical and training advice. Dr. Sargent's knowledge helped to substantiate much of the information on stretching, self-care and training.

My thanks to Nike for unwavering support and encouragement since I first broke onto the running scene in the late 1970s. Nike hasn't missed a stride since that time, and I fully expect that we both have many strides ahead of us. At Nike I would personally like to thank Alberto Salazar, John Notar, Tom Hartge and Mary Ellen Smith for the help and information they provided for the book.

Thanks also to nutrition researcher Jaime S. Rudd in Lincoln, Nebraska, Henley Gibble, executive director of the Road Runners Club of America, exercise science professor LaJean Lawson, Ph.D., at Oregon State University in Corvallis and elite runner Francie Larrieu Smith.

Sharon Faelten and Lee Jackson, our editors at Rodale Press, have been at every mile marker during this marathon of writing. Their passion and ability, coupled with their personal involvement and enthusiasm as women runners themselves, helped ensure this book would touch runners of all abilities and backgrounds. Many thanks to them both for their patience and hard work and for making sure this book is nothing short of complete.

Amby Burfoot and Claire Kowalchik of *Runner's World* magazine reviewed the manuscript in the early stages and offered many helpful comments and suggestions.

My thanks to runners everywhere for their support and for sharing with me the sport that gives us all fulfillment and inner peace no matter what the pace of our lives.

Last, but certainly not least, my loving thanks to my family: Scott, Abby and Anders, for their unconditional love and support. They have given me a "run" that will last a lifetime.

—*Joan Samuelson*

INTRODUCTION

The numbers are in and they show women's running is hot. For a sport that's experiencing such a boom, it would seem the literature is abundant. Far from it. It's been almost a decade since a book on women's running was published. One of the last books published was my own *The Woman Runner—Free to Be the Complete Athlete*, so you might expect me to begin by saying how much things have changed. But I think the theme of my last book on women's running still applies: the need for women to define ourselves as athletes.

I believe that by living as athletes we live more fully. Our sport becomes not just what we do but an integral symbol—on all levels—of who we are. When we understand the privilege of what it means to be an athlete, we are in touch with, and rejoice in, our physical, mental and emotional strengths and our endless possibilities. As athletes—even just by who we are and how we live—we are able to pass on a great gift to other women and girls.

In the beginning, you likely say, "I run." With more confidence you say, "I am a runner." After reading this book, many will say, "I am an athlete."

To this end, the focus of this book is on taking your sport a step further—by developing not only your running but your athleticism. This is reflected in cutting-edge training, drills, diet, lifestyle and medical advice. The totality of this advice is illustrated by its range. It comes from both Joan Samuelson and the best experts in various fields, and it is for runners from under 10 to over 40 and beyond.

Joan Samuelson is in a unique position to highlight the themes of this book. As an Olympic gold medalist and mother of two, she has learned to focus intensely on her sport and to balance her love of running with her love of motherhood. Balance—in sport, career, family and all of life—is the key theme of our lives in the 1990s, and it is Joan's primary personal theme and her theme in this book.

Joan is a world-class athlete in touch with the most important aspects of physical endurance and perseverance and of striving to realize a dream despite any obstacles. From her outstanding efforts to compete in the 1984 Olympics and to win the gold to her adamant decision to combine her training with child care—she is a woman who gets the best from herself because she believes in her ability to reach the top. In all endeavors, she exemplifies the go-for-it attitude. She has imbued this book with the practical advice and winning attitude you need to take it to the limit.

I hope that when you close the covers of this book, you will hit the road equipped with the knowledge, confidence and inspiration to go as far and as fast as you possibly can.

—Gloria Averbuch

PART I

RUNNING ADVICE
FOR WOMEN

CHAPTER 1

WHY RUN?

Everyone Has a Reason

Years ago, women sat in kitchens drinking coffee and discussing life. Today, they cover the same topics while they run. Why? For many reasons. The psychological and physical benefits vary. Some enjoy the increased confidence, energy, muscle and bone strength, endurance and cardiovascular health that running bestows. Others run because of what running helps them lower—their weight, blood pressures, resting heart rates, anxiety and depression. Some run for more than one reason; some started running for one reason and continue for another, or their goals and needs change.

Speaking for myself, I run for the love of it and for all it does for me, from the ability to compete against others and against myself to the calming day-in, day-out training routine that is part of both my physical and mental health.

Sometimes it seems odd to say I run for a living. I guess I'm still wondering what I'm going to do when I "grow up." When I was in college, I attended career seminars, assuming the next logical step after graduation was a teaching job or graduate school. At about the same time, I was beginning to have success on the national and international scene. Major wins, including the 1979 Boston Marathon, and invitations to competitions around the world more than filled my schedule. It was at this time that I decided to devote myself to full-time training and racing.

I promised myself that if and when I no longer found running enjoyable and rewarding, I'd stop. Years later, I'm still at it; I still love it, and I continue to look forward to achieving my running goals. My love of running is a feeling every woman can experience.

The Making of an Athlete: Challenges and Role Models

I've been running regularly since I was 15 years old. From my first race on a grade school ball field, running has provided a challenge— even to today, when I am contemplating trying out for the 1996 Olympic team.

Various factors nurtured my athletic ability. I am the third of four children and the only girl. My two older brothers are successful runners, and my parents are also very athletic. In addition, I'm a native of Maine, where a tradition of a strong work ethic and love of the outdoors prevails.

Like most young children, my dreams changed daily. But my love of sports kept at least one of those dreams alive. I was a tomboy and dreamed of going to the Olympics.

My entire family skied, and for a time, I aspired to become world class in that sport. Growing up with three brothers tested my strength and tenacity. As a child, I would ski through the toughest weather or under the most challenging conditions to prove I could endure the elements as long as any of my brothers. This early experience paved the way for working passionately toward a goal.

Like most people, I had my share of role models—people I admired or looked to for inspiration and who kept me motivated. I think most of us can look back at our childhood and remember the impact others made on our future choices. Watching my brothers run was one source of inspiration. Certain coaches and teachers also inspired me. Their enthusiasm ignited my drive to succeed—both on the track and in the classroom. The first high-school girl in Maine to run with any success was a miler named Brook Merrow. I really looked up to her. Today, she's a running mom, and we share a strong friendship.

In the professional arena, female runners like Francie Larrieu Smith and Mary Decker Slaney provided early motivation. Credit also goes to peers like Grete Waitz and Ingrid Kristiansen. I admire Priscilla Welch as an athlete and a breast cancer survivor. Now I look to Olympic medalist Lynn Jennings and Anne Marie Letko and the next generation of women runners.

Many women runners have told me of the wonderful, supportive friendships they have built as training partners. I think we should all seek out role models, and not only runners. Whether the role models we choose work in politics, the arts or entertainment, we all know that feeling of admiration of others that fuels us at various—often meaningful—times.

The Running Life

I run as early in the morning as I possibly can, before the day comes into full swing. My running gives me a chance to "air out" problems or plans. I review my schedule and prioritize the day. Sometimes I visualize an upcoming race—particularly if it's a big one.

An early run allows me to feel good about myself for the rest of the day and to get my "fix." Coffee doesn't do it for me; it's running that gets me going. If I haven't had my run, I'm irritable. I feel sluggish and inept in dealing with daily activities. After I run, I feel I can deal with just about anything that comes my way—whether it's a business call, getting my daughter out the door to school, keeping my son amused or all of them simultaneously.

Life is truly a balancing act. In one hand, you hold your running, and in the other, you hold your job, family and other tasks and challenges that you face on a daily basis. For all the things that are important in your life, you have to find that balance.

With all I do in my life, I'm still trying to keep my balance. It's an endless challenge. Balance is a key theme in this book, because it has become a key theme in every aspect of my life as well as in the lives of so many women I know. In fact, when the Melpomene Institute for Women's Health Research in St. Paul, a well-respected, nonprofit organization that does extensive research on women's health and physical activity, asked women what, if anything, kept them from running as much as they'd like to, the number-one obstacle named was lack of time because of workplace demands followed by lack of time because of family responsibilities.

Only you can decide how to create a harmonious balance. Ultimately, only you know your body, your psyche and the demands in your life. It may take a while to find that balance, but you'll know when it's achieved. And when you do, it's like a good race, like the runner's high.

What Works for *You*

One of the early lessons I learned as an athlete is the need for flexibility, which is another important theme of the training advice in this book. Athletics, like everything else, is a trial-and-error process. You stay with what works, you discard what doesn't. That's why flexibility is an important ingredient in any training program.

This has always been true in my career but perhaps nothing has tested that truth like my two children: my seven-year-old daughter, Abigail, and five-year-old son, Anders. Since they were born, I've had to change my training radically (and subsequently, often my goals). In doing so, I have learned that some things work and some don't. When Abby was born, for example, I thought I could continue to train twice a day. But I was just digging myself into a hole. After a few weeks of sleep deprivation and frequent feedings, I had to give up that second run (except on track workout days). It is a change that has remained permanent. Now I work to make my one run a day a quality run.

If you're not flexible when you start out, it's a trait you acquire by necessity. Before children—B.C. I call it—I would have said I could never be satisfied unless I ran twice a day at least five days a week. Cutting back, however, left me energized, not fatigued; renewed, not burned out. That's the beauty of this sport—it's adaptable.

No doubt about it, combining an athletic career with motherhood definitely has its ups and downs. To do well at both, I have established my own personal set of priorities. For any woman runner, priorities determine how you spend your time, attention and energy. I do tend to become more focused, and a bit more selfish, when I'm training for a major race, for example. For the most part, other than the one to three hours of my training time—and barring meetings or travel—I spend my time with my children.

Another important theme of this book—which is true for both training and lifestyle—is developing a sense of wholeness. Unless you feel happy about yourself, as integrated as possible, you can't expect to have success in anything—from running to mothering to any other job. I cannot stress enough how great an effect this has had on both my personal and professional life.

There's not a better feeling than when you have found that moment of balance and harmony when both running and life come together. Then you truly know why you run and that you couldn't live without it.

CHAPTER 2

SIZE, STRENGTH AND STAMINA

Women versus Men

Equal playing fields: Women are achieving equality in the workplace, in school and in the home. But what about a playing field itself—the track? When people start comparing men and women runners, Joan likes to tell a story about a couple she knows: "They're both recreational runners who do it for pleasure and fitness. They run together and even race against each other, and it's always the same: She beats him every time."

Are women runners any different from men who run? The answer seems to be a resounding yes—and no. Yes, because certain physical differences can and do affect performance. Across the board, men log faster times than women. But at the same time, women runners can (and do) train and race like men. So will we—can we—catch up?

As an elite runner, Joan had a unique opportunity to play a role in the scientific study of male and female runners and how they differ.

In 1983, she participated in research conducted by noted exercise physiologist Jack Daniels, Ph.D., head cross-country and track coach for men and women at the State University of New York at Cortland. Dr. Daniels conducted a test of 30 elite women distance runners at the Nike laboratory in Exeter, New Hampshire. Joan was his assistant as well as a participant in the study. In 1991, studies involved male and female runners who were in training for the U.S. Olympic trials.

Using the findings in his studies, along with others, we'll compare some basic physical traits—size, maximal oxygen capacity (VO_2 max), running efficiency and body composition—and see how men and women measure up.

Is Bigger Better?

No question about it, men are bigger. In other words, they are, on average, taller, have a greater stride length and weigh more. Is that why they're faster? If it were, the biggest person in every race would win. No, size and strength alone don't account for higher speeds. The real cause is hormones—the force behind size and strength.

It's pretty basic, really: Men produce copious amounts of testosterone, the sex hormone that, among other things, increases the concentration of red blood cells and promotes the production of hemoglobin, the protein that carries oxygen within red blood cells. Estrogen, the hormone that predominates in women, does not have this effect. To emphasize this difference, Owen Anderson, Ph.D., technical editor for *Runner's World* magazine, gives a vivid example: "Each liter of a man's blood contains 150 to 160 grams of hemoglobin—20 grams more hemoglobin and 11 percent more oxygen than the average for women."

Although a man's running ability is generally superior to a woman's, there is a tremendous area of overlap, says Dr. Daniels. He points out that although the best male runner outperforms the best female, "very few men are better than the best women runners." In fact, many women runners—regardless of their levels—can turn around after the finish of a race and see the legions of men they have bettered. So, obviously, other factors come into play.

How We Measure Up

The study conducted by Dr. Daniels did not measure hormone levels per se. It did, however, chart two key barometers of running ability: maximal oxygen capacity (VO_2 max), which measures the greatest volume of oxygen that can be dispatched to your muscles during exercise, and running economy, which he defines as how much work goes into running at a specific speed. Together, these two distinctive elements further determine running ability.

In running, VO_2 max determines how far you can run more than how fast you can run. If you think about it, it makes sense, since by definition VO_2 max measures the volume of oxygen per unit of body weight over time (milliliters/kilograms/minutes).

Dr. Daniels tested Joan and others for VO_2 max by having them run on a treadmill at increasing degrees of incline until exhaustion. The higher the VO_2 max, the better the individual was able to use the oxygen that was delivered to the running muscles. Dr. Daniels explains: "Think of your body as a car. The carburetor mixes air and fuel and sends it to the engine. You can pour extra gas in, but if the engine can't accept it, it's of no use."

VO_2 Max: Not the Whole Story

Take a look at these world-class runners and compare their VO_2 max measurements with their marathon times. As you can see, Joan Samuelson's VO_2 max is about the same as two other male champions, but her best marathon time is more than ten minutes slower. Similarly, legendary distance runner Derek Clayton tested at a VO_2 max of 69.0 but clocked in ahead of rivals who tested higher. Bottom line: Running economy made the difference. With more economical running and perhaps a more efficient running style that saved extra energy, an athlete can get farther on the same tank of gas (O_2). Obviously, Derek Clayton doesn't need as much oxygen to race at nearly the same speed as Alberto Salazar.

So what determines an individual's VO_2 max? As you might guess, genetics plays a role. But it is also strongly related to a characteristic mentioned earlier: the hemoglobin content of the blood. Because of their higher concentration of red blood cells, says Dr. Daniels, men's muscles seem to be able to process more oxygen, and, thus, men have the potential for higher VO_2 max values.

In test after test, Dr. Daniels found that, in general, women runners tend to have a VO_2 max 10 to 12 percent lower than men. But there are some notable exceptions—and Joan is one of them. When Dr. Daniels assessed Joan's VO_2 max, she tested at 78—higher than most elite men runners. In fact, while these athletes were running at about 88 percent of capacity, Joan's VO_2 max was identical to former marathon-world-record-holder Alberto Salazar.

Running Economics 101

Why, then, is Alberto Salazar faster than Joan Samuelson? That's where running economy comes in. To test this, Dr. Daniels had Joan, Alberto and other world-class runners run on a level treadmill at six increasing speeds to assess the amount of energy used at each given

Runner	VO₂ Max (ml/kg/min)	Best Marathon Time
Bill Rodgers	78.5	2:09:27
Alberto Salazar	78.0	2:08:13
Joan Samuelson	78.0	2:21:21
Grete Waitz	73.0	2:25:29
Frank Shorter	71.3	2:10:30
Derek Clayton	69.0	2:08:33

pace. On the treadmill, as on the marathon course, Salazar won hands down. Why? Better running economy.

In other words, at various speeds some runners use oxygen more economically than others. Because Salazar used less oxygen at these given speeds, his running proved to be far more efficient than Joan's. To recall the car fuel analogy, he got more miles per gallon.

Form, or running style, also affects how efficiently you run. How your arms move, how much bounce is in your step and those little side-to-side moves and corrections to balance done automatically—all play a part in how much energy you burn. The less vertical move-ment—in other words, the less you bounce up and down as you run—the more efficient your gait. According to Ned Frederick, Ph.D., former director of research at Nike, the most efficient runners glide along with very little vertical movement.

Can running economy be altered? On this score, men and women are equal. With speed training, says Dr. Daniels, economy can be im-proved significantly, much like aerobic capacity. The same is true of form. To a degree, each body automatically finds its best form with time and experience.

And one other factor exerts a great deal of influence: the baggage you carry with you.

Keep the Muscle, Lose the Fat

Say an exercise physiologist like Dr. Daniels tested two runners who were fairly equal in size, training, oxygen capacity and running economy, but asked one of them to carry a backpack with weights in it. Who would have the advantage? Obviously, the unencumbered in-dividual would be the odds-on favorite. Thus, we find a real advantage to running with less fat weighing down your muscles.

When it comes to percentage of body fat, not all is equal between the sexes. As a group, men have proportionately more muscle and women have more fat—that's part of the equipment nature gives women to bear children. This goes back to the testosterone-estrogen equation. The average athletic guy has a percentage of body fat ranging anywhere from 8 to 20 percent; for the average athletic woman, 13 to 25 percent is the norm. (These numbers can be much higher for folks who are overweight or out of shape.)

BODY FAT: MORE IS LESS

At one time, some running experts (most notably, Joan Ullyot, M.D., a well-known runner and sports medicine expert) suggested that additional body fat might give women an advantage in distance racing, especially beyond a marathon. The theory was that women runners could draw on their fat reserves to push them beyond long-distance limits. As popular as this notion may be, it has not proved to be the case.

"Metabolizing fat as a fuel source is not as economical as metabolizing carbohydrates. Burning fat requires more oxygen," says Jack Daniels, Ph.D., noted exercise physiologist and head cross-country and track coach for men and women at the State University of New York at Cortland. "Maybe fat would pay off if the average man and woman were stranded in the wilderness and neither had food, but stored fat is not necessarily an advantage during exercise."

In general, for athletes of comparable ability, women will have twice the percentage of body fat than their male counterparts—about 6 to 13 percent versus 3 to 8 percent for men. Thus, a 125-pound woman tends to be slightly "fatter," with less lean-muscle mass, than a man who weighs the same. Her extra fat increases the energy cost of any physical effort, making running even more laborious. The added ration of fat affects all types of exercise but is theoretically a real disadvantage in running, where the body weight is carried by the athlete.

Body fat isn't the only factor slowing women down, but it's a big factor. If body fat levels were more equal, racing times between men and women might also be closer. Russell Pate, Ph.D., an exercise physiologist at the University of South Carolina in Columbia, tested 16 men and women who were similarly trained and had the same VO_2 max values and the same body fat percentages (17 percent). He had them run a 15-mile race, and they finished just about even.

Just because a woman inherently carries more fat doesn't mean she can't trim it down, even to the level of a man. Women can change their body composition quite a bit. As weight goes down, oxygen uptake improves, says Robert Vaughan, Ph.D., exercise physiologist at Baylor University Medical Center in Dallas. But that doesn't necessarily mean women should reduce their body fat. At a certain point, the cost of getting thinner or staying thin becomes detrimental to health and running ability. "Many women who try to reduce to extremely low body fat levels become amenorrheic, losing their menstrual periods," says Dr. Vaughan. Statistics show that they also tend to have more injuries, particularly stress fractures.

The questions are: What's safe and what's reasonable? Of the 30 elite women runners Dr. Daniels tested, he also measured body fat. He reports that Joan was one of the "fatter ones" (imagine the overall levels if Joan is a scant 11.3 percent). "The fact that Joan has competed so long and so successfully and did not lose her menstrual cycle during training suggests that her body kept a healthy balance at that weight and fat level," notes Dr. Vaughan.

Joan has a very compact body—unlike many other elite runners, she's not overly lean or tall and willowy with a long stride. She's petite and carries around 105 pounds on her small frame. Yet, all the numbers and measurements aside, she was born with an innate genetic ability, which she has developed to its greatest potential.

So, Joan doesn't encourage women runners to strive for super low body fat in hopes of improving their running performance. She makes the point, "At 8 percent body fat, a man who runs may be at his strongest and may be very successful at running, while a woman at 8 percent may be compromised. That might be too low for her to maintain a healthy balance and stay strong. We need to realize what healthy parameters are."

Like most experts, Dr. Daniels and Dr. Vaughan are adamantly opposed to the quest for unhealthy thinness. Joan's achievements, when looked at within the context of elite women runners, Dr. Daniels says, prove you don't have to starve yourself to be successful.

Women runners who strive and struggle to reach unnaturally low weights may have great motivation, Dr. Daniels believes, but probably don't have as much genetic ability as some others. It is these women who college coaches like Dr. Daniels watch out for—to see that they don't do themselves harm. Joan agrees and cautions, "There are a few coaches, however, who may encourage this extreme attitude, but it would be healthier to promote the idea that all body types are good."

A Better Way to Catch Up

One healthier way for women to close the performance gap between men and women is through resistance training, says Dr. Daniels. It's a sure way for women to build more muscle and lose fat. And you don't have to bulk up to unnatural proportions, nor should you. "You pay a price for carrying extra body weight, whether it be fat or muscle," cautions Dr. Daniels. (See page 148 for more information on resistance training for women.)

Vive la Différence

Men and women are different, and so are male and female athletes. Along with minor variations, basic physical differences prevail. A good strategy for a woman runner may be to compete for herself first, against other women second and then against men if she wants to.

"I want to emphasize that the differences between men and women stem from their separate strengths," says Joan. "Let's remember, our bodies have many functions, and running is just one of many uplifting experiences of our physical existence."

CHAPTER 3

FROM PMS TO MENOPAUSE

How Women Runners Cope

Aside from gender-based differences in body composition, hormones and so forth, women runners have other unique biological concerns. You menstruate. (Or don't, but should. Or used to.) You have children. (Or want to. Or don't want to.) Your body produces certain hormones (like estrogen), at least until menopause, when it produces less. Unless, of course, you take oral estrogen to make up the difference.

Add the fact that women have their own nutritional requirements, and it's no surprise that, if you're a runner, exercise is going to toss another factor into the mix (for the good, we might add).

At 38, Joan doesn't anticipate experiencing the changes associated with menopause for some time. But like most women runners, she has had her share of menstrual phenomena, including mood swings, bloating and food cravings. She hasn't let it get in her way, however. Joan's period was due the day of the 1984 Olympic Marathon and she won.

Since that victory, she's had two pregnancies and ran during both of them. Here, Joan tells how menstruation, premenstrual syndrome and other womanly concerns have affected her running, how other women runners may be affected, how she's coped and what the women doctors she's consulted have to say. Topics covered include:

- Cramps
- Bloating
- Mood swings
- Food cravings
- PMS
- Menstruation
- Amenorrhea (absence of menstruation)
- Birth control
- Vaginitis
- Bladder problems
- Endometriosis
- Menopause

Periodic Peaks and Valleys

If you've ever watched top women race, you may have wondered what happens to them if they get their periods on race day. How do serious women runners cope with PMS, tampons and cramps and still do their best? For that matter, how does menstruation and the associated changes affect day-to-day training?

One of the great benefits of running on any level is that it develops a keen sense of the body and its natural rhythms. Any change, including menstruation, affects the way you train and race. So women who are serious about exercise want to anticipate the waves of physical and emotional changes throughout the month.

Several ways your body changes during your period include:

Cramps. First, be assured that menstrual cramps are normal—a sign that the body is working properly. This doesn't mean the discomfort has to interfere with your workout.

Over-the-counter medications like ibuprofen (Advil, Motrin and Nuprin) can and do relieve menstrual cramps. Ibuprofen works by blocking the formation of prostaglandins, naturally occurring substances that cause painful uterine contractions (cramping). Most women need a pain reliever for only the first day or two of menstruation, according to women runners and doctors Joan has consulted.

The dosage in over-the-counter ibuprofen is lower than prescription medication, but doctors say that may be enough for most women. If not, ask your physician about a higher dosage of over-the-counter drugs or other medications, some available by prescription, like naproxen (Anaprox, Naprosyn) or Ponstel. These anti-inflammatory medications also inhibit the production of prostaglandins. They're more potent and deliver higher dosages, however. Any of these medications can cause stomach upset, although taking them with food often wards off the problem.

Menstrual cramps and pain aren't inevitable, of course. If you're like a lot of women, you may find that your periods are less bothersome since taking up an exercise like running. According to Constance LeBrun, M.D., professor in the Department of Family Practice at the University of British Columbia in Vancouver, active women report fewer menstrual cramps and headaches, suffer less lower-back pain, anxiety, depression and fatigue and use fewer painkillers.

Bloating. Feelings of fullness can be especially frustrating for women runners; it's even worse if your legs also feel heavy, particularly while running. Almost any part of the body—including the abdomen, feet, ankles and breasts—can retain fluid and swell before menstruation.

When Joan feels bloated before her period, she drinks more water. Although you'd think the last thing you need is more fluid, Mona Shangold, M.D., noted author and sports medicine gynecologist at Hahnemann University Hospital in Philadelphia, confirms that drinking water helps. Swelling is a sign of sodium retention, points out Dr. Shangold. Taking more fluids helps flush out the excess sodium and alleviates the feeling of bloating.

"Many women who feel bloated do the opposite of what they should. They don't drink, and they end up retaining fluid," says Dr. Shangold. A low-sodium diet during the week leading up to menstruation helps to alleviate bloating. Her advice: Avoid salty snacks, processed foods and table salt, the primary sources of excess sodium in the diet. Joan adds, "Many runners drink sodas with a surprisingly high level of sodium. So check the labels on the bottles."

Mood swings. The menstrual cycle can play havoc with your emotions, causing depression and edginess. Exercise can ease the mood swings that some women experience during their menstrual cycles. One study in the *British Journal of Sportsmedicine* found that, overall, runners had milder premenstrual symptoms and better moods than inactive women.

PMS MUNCHIES

It's a day or two before your period, and you just can't stop snacking—chocolate chip cookies after breakfast, a muffin later in the day and a serious longing for a candy bar before bed.

What woman hasn't experienced premenstrual munchies? These food cravings may be related to hormonal changes. According to Nancy Clark, R.D., noted nutrition author and nutritional consultant at Sportsmedicine in Brookline, Massachusetts, a woman's higher metabolic rate during this time may, in fact, cause an increase in nutritional needs of 200 to 500 calories (the equivalent of an extra meal). This hunger tends to hit in the form of cravings for sweets.

Clark points out, however, that women athletes—who are notably weight conscious—may try to fight these food urges, especially if they also feel heavy from premenstrual bloating. Don't fight the munchies, advises Clark. Instead, try to control moods and cravings by adding more carbohydrate calories at breakfast and lunch. This will help curtail the premenstrual syndrome sugar urge. Eating carbohydrates may also help improve PMS moods, like depression, adds Mona Shangold, M.D., noted author and sports medicine gynecologist at Hahnemann University Hospital in Philadelphia.

Diet can also affect your moods—which brings us to the next subject: food.

Food cravings. One rule Joan has made for herself is this: Don't fight food cravings. But she doesn't abandon herself to those cravings, either. If she overdoes it with junk food, for example, her running feels flat. She tends to crave chocolate, which she eats in moderation. To keep her blood sugar even, especially at the menstrual point in her cycle, Joan tends to eat more snacks or small meals as opposed to fewer large meals.

Tampon Tactics

You may be worried about heavy menstrual flow while running during your period, particularly in a race. And with just cause. Menstrual bleeding may increase during exercise, says Dr. Shangold.

As it happens, though, most women don't overflow while running or racing. Those who prefer a sense of security pack a tampon or pad in case there's an opportunity to stop and change or use a pre-race portable toilet. (Some enlightened race organizers stock tampons in the portable toilets.) Joan has been known to carry a tampon in a plastic bag pinned inside her running shorts—she did it in the Olympics.

Other solutions: Use a super-absorbency tampon or—Dr. Shangold's two personal preferences—a panty liner with a tampon or a diaphragm with a tampon.

One of the benefits, according to Dr. Shangold, of drugs designed to alleviate menstrual cramps (such as ibuprofen) is that they reduce menstrual bleeding. This helps to calm the worry of bleeding during exercise. Losing less blood also lowers the risk of iron deficiency.

Menstruation and Marathons

Joan sees a parallel between her menstrual cycle and the athletic experience. "For me, PMS means more than premenstrual syndrome—it could also stand for something I call premarathon syndrome. Both the physical and emotional feelings are similar: irritability, mood swings and energy drain. And they can be equally severe.

"Among my women running friends, we talk about the M word,

which stands for both menstruation and marathon. These events are the culmination of physical and emotional cycles. Because I do equate these experiences, I've always felt it would be interesting to study the similarities between marathon training and the menstrual cycle—and how they might interact and affect one another.

"During certain phases in my cycle, I find I can't always concen-

JOAN'S STRATEGIES FOR RUNNING DURING YOUR PERIOD

Here are some strategies from Joan and her consultants for dealing with menstrual discomforts when you run.

Cramps. Lightly stretching or exercising the abdominal area can help relax cramping and improves blood flow to the site. To stretch her abdomen, Joan bends backward while standing. As an alternative, you can do bent-knee situps, says Joan.

Bloating. Drink large amounts of water and avoid salty foods. Fruit juices, which contain potassium, also help to release water and excess sodium from your tissues. Be aware that many sodas are high in sodium. Be sure to empty your bladder before running, especially if you're drinking a lot of fluids.

Mood swings. Joan is especially affected by mood swings during her period. If she feels grumpy, exercise generally picks her up. She finds she often loses that irritability during a run. A good, hard workout can release negative or stressful feelings.

Energy drain. Eating sweets can give you a temporary surge, only to be followed by a crash. Instead, eat several small meals high in complex carbohydrates to help boost energy. Fig bars, sandwiches and the like can help keep you on an even keel.

Don't make the mistake of attributing a sluggish run to poor training. If you have an "off" training day during your period, don't blame yourself—just ride it out. Better times are often just ahead.

trate. And physically, I feel a bit 'off.' I try to deal with it by telling my-self, 'This, too, shall pass.' My advice: Don't lose your focus. Remind yourself that you've faced obstacles or distractions in the past, and you've overcome them."

Running during Menstruation

A runner gearing up for a race wants to know what phase of her cycle will be in play on the big day. Joan finds that keeping a running log or diary can help. Along with your training notes, include any physical changes and emotional moods related to your period. By charting high- and low-energy levels and negative and positive train-ing or racing results, you will better understand your personal cycles. This way you can ride out the tough times and work on the big game plan, such as choosing a marathon. Charting your diet can also help you discover which foods and drinks work best for you.

Don't condition yourself by thinking that you may not run well during a particular time of the month. Women have won Olympic gold medals during all phases of their cycles. Joan feels strongly about this. "If I'm focused on a big race and expecting PMS or my period, the adrenaline from my excitement takes over and wipes out any neg-ative feelings. My period becomes inconsequential—a peripheral event.

"When it comes to the effect of your cycle on your running, my motto is: Go with your feelings and instincts. Most of my training is based on a firm week-by-week plan, but, if I feel I can't stick to it one particular day because of my period, I adapt and, if necessary, I cut back. Menstruation, when it's difficult, may also be a good time to cross train. Trying a different activity can help you feel less tired, so it may be easier to get through the workout.

"One thing I don't recommend is completely canceling a run dur-ing a rough physical or emotional patch. Even if I feel down, I go out to run. In my experience, even an easy run will usually elevate my mood. Besides, you can't shut down for one to two weeks every month. And there may come a time when it is not possible to adapt your running, such as a scheduled race. It is better not to limit your-self—learn to run at every time of the month."

Sometimes your period is due at just the wrong time—whether it's a job interview or a racing event. Every once in a while, by sheer force of will it seems, the cycle resets itself, and it misses the scheduled start.

The mind/body connection is truly remarkable. Joan recalls, "In the 1984 Olympics, my period was scheduled to start on race day. I believe I was actually able, by mental will, to delay it by one day. In fact, several times during major competitions my period has started early or late." Although she cannot confirm or deny the power of the mind to delay menstruation for competition, Dr. Shangold feels it would make an interesting study. "There certainly is a mind/body connection," she asserts. "The brain dictates how and when the endocrine glands release chemicals that affect other parts of the body. We know that stress, for example, can affect the menstrual cycle. Changes in training can also affect the menstrual cycle."

When You Don't Get Your Period

Recently, a study found that one of every five serious women runners is amenorrheic—they don't menstruate. And in a medical forum for active and athletic women, Lori Marshall, M.D., clinical instructor in the Department of Obstetrics and Gynecology at the University of Washington School of Medicine in Seattle, reported that nearly half of all elite women runners no longer get their periods.

Although a direct cause has not been found, amenorrhea in these athletes seems to stem from a complex set of factors. Intense training, often accompanied by an inadequate diet, lowers body fat levels and consequently, estrogen production diminishes. When there's little or no estrogen, periods almost always stop.

For women who find menstruation a bother, losing periods might sound like good news, but it's not. Women who stop menstruating for long stretches of time during their reproductive years may have trouble conceiving, since ovulation stops when periods lapse. Other long-range consequences may include premature osteoporosis (bone loss) and a greater risk of heart disease because of estrogen deficiency.

Women who stop menstruating also have a higher risk of stress fractures, a common running-related injury. Studies indicate that 50 percent of amenorrheic women runners sustain stress fractures, compared with about 30 percent of runners with normal periods. So, while menstruation may seem inconvenient, a woman is better off menstruating than not.

Despite strenuous training, Joan rarely missed a period. "The only time I ever missed my period was in my first three years of college but only during the academic year. It returned during semester breaks and in the summer. My experience is not typical since I weighed more and had a higher percentage of body fat when I didn't menstruate than when I did. Although amenorrhea is generally believed to be brought on by hard training, in my case, I would guess it had more to do with the emotional stress I felt during that time."

Women runners who begin training intensely may suddenly stop menstruating. But some of these same women may also binge then starve or exercise to excess, or both, in order to achieve unrealistic (and unhealthy) super-low body weights. Doctors call loss of periods from training athletic amenorrhea.

John Babington, coach at the Liberty Athletic Club for 19 years and assistant coach for the 1996 Olympic women's track-and-field team, notices two distinct types among his successful runners: The athlete who excels with no significant change in her weight or period, and the athlete who achieves a high level of performance only after she becomes very lean and often amenorrheic.

Researcher Alice K. Lindeman, R.D., from the University of Indiana in Bloomington, claims that the women who binge and exercise to excess are trying to overcompensate. Genetically, they tend to be lesser equipped to run fast or far, but they want to perform like the naturally gifted athletes, so they go to extremes.

Robert Vaughan, Ph.D., an exercise physiologist at Baylor University Medical Center in Dallas, kept a watchful eye on the women's 10-K race in the 1993 national track-and-field championships. He noticed that the top three finishers were "lean but not unhealthy in their appearance." Trailing them, he said, "were a group that appeared to be unnaturally thin and were struggling to run with the top women."

Why Women Athletes Need Enough Calories

The more intensely you train and the lower your body fat, the more likely you are to miss your period and run the risk of fractures and other harmful consequences. To restore the normal balance in your menstrual cycle, some experts recommend curtailing your training and allowing yourself to gain a few pounds. Dr. Marshall advises a cutback in training of 5 to 15 percent and a small weight gain of 2 to 3 percent of body weight. If you weigh 110 pounds, that's 2.2 to 3.3 pounds.

You don't, however, need to cut back on your workouts, says Dr. Shangold. "A nutritionist may help you analyze your weight and diet to see if you are eating enough and properly for the amount of calories burned by exercise." She recommends that women who miss periods see a gynecologist to be sure there are no medical causes. Very often, she says, women who have missed their periods for six months or more should be treated with hormones to replace what is not being made by the body. Although many athletes hesitate to take hormones, Dr. Shangold feels treatment is important to prevent the loss of bone mass from estrogen deficiency.

Across the board, nutritionists and other health professionals urge amenorrheic women to upgrade their eating habits. They need more calories, more protein and more calcium, not rigid super-low-fat deprivation diets. Like Dr. Shangold, Nancy Clark, noted nutrition author and nutritional consultant at Sportsmedicine in Brookline, Massachusetts, believes that poor nutrition, more than training, may be a key factor in causing amenorrhea. The long-range consequences? Osteoporosis. And the last thing any athletic woman wants is brittle bones.

So serious are these nutritional concerns that in June 1992, the American College of Sports Medicine in Indianapolis assembled a panel of experts to discuss the growing problem of exercise-related amenorrhea among adolescent and young adult women athletes. Kimberly L. Yeager, M.D., assistant director of Public Health Practice at San Diego State University, coined the term *female athlete triad* to describe the combination of amenorrhea, osteoporosis and disordered eating in young women athletes who are training intensely. (For more on the problem of eating disorders, see page 170.)

No Periods, No Pregnancy?

Not surprisingly, if your exercise program includes long or heavy workouts and you've missed periods, you could have problems getting pregnant when you want to. "Amenorrheic athletes are usually infertile while their periods are absent," says Dr. Shangold, "but most can become pregnant with hormone treatment."

Still, hormone treatments are serious business—a last resort. Before seeking treatment, women who can't seem to get pregnant may prefer to lessen the intensity of their exercise and try to gain weight in an attempt to rekindle ovulation. "You should consult a fertility expert," says Dr. Shangold, "to determine the cause of the problem. Most infertility problems have nothing to do with exercise."

Don't Ignore Birth Control

Some women consider not having a period as a method of birth control. But when periods are about to resume, the first ovulation often occurs before menstrual bleeding. So if you don't want to conceive and aren't menstruating, it's a good idea to use birth control anyway, just to be safe.

Does the fact that you run have any bearing on your method of birth control? In the early 1980s, several studies found that among women runners using birth control the diaphragm was the method of choice for most. The Melpomene Institute for Women's Health Research in St. Paul, a well-respected, nonprofit organization that does extensive research on women's health and physical activity, conducted a survey that indicates that over time, fewer women runners are using diaphragms and IUDs, while more are using condoms. Together, barrier methods are the most popular choices (condoms, diaphragms and foam choices equaled 53.1 percent). In contrast, nonrunners seem to prefer oral contraceptives (30.7 percent), while only a small percentage of survey respondents (11 percent) chose this method.

When it comes right down to it, no method of birth control seems to have any particular advantage or disadvantage for women runners. In one of the few studies of birth control and athletic performance in women, Dr. LeBrun reported no significant changes in an athlete's performance from taking the pill. She did detect small decreases in VO_2 max (maximal oxygen capacity), suggesting that taking the pill may slightly reduce aerobic capacity. The study indicates, though, that unless you're an elite athlete, your own performance will not be greatly affected.

Before the 1984 Olympic Games, many women competitors talked among themselves about taking hormones to alter the timing of their menstrual cycles. They asked Joan if she, too, planned to get a prescription. "I'm not comfortable altering my cycle," says Joan, "so I said no. Besides, I reasoned that I had run during my period before, so I could do it again."

Running with Infections

"Most women will have at least one infection of the genital or reproductive tract during their lives," says Dr. Shangold. "Some have problems on a regular basis. Running doesn't cause any of them, and in most cases, women can continue to exercise." She has this to say about some common gynecological infections.

Vaginitis (yeast infections). Vaginitis is an infection of the vagina by yeasts such as Candida or Trichomonas. Symptoms include vaginal itching, discharge or odor. Yeast infections are so common that the medications doctors use to treat them are sold over the counter. If these don't help, however, see your gynecologist.

Exercise does not cause a yeast infection. But if you run, the combination of heat, sweat and friction can make the discomfort maddening. Be sure to wear clothing that is not too tight and is made of natural fabrics that breathe, like cotton. Shorts or loose pants will promote ventilation, which lets sweat evaporate rather than irritate.

Bladder infections. A burning sensation while urinating or a frequent urge to urinate calls for medical treatment. See a doctor. If the cause is a bacterial infection, she will prescribe three to five days of antibiotics. You should feel relief by the second day, perhaps even sooner. Continue to take the pills until they're all gone.

At the onset, running with a bladder infection may be uncomfortable, but, again, exercise does not cause this problem or make a woman susceptible to it. Incidentally, feeling the need to urinate frequently does not indicate the actual presence of urine. The feeling is caused by an irritated bladder.

Herpes. An outbreak of genital herpes can be extremely painful, making it uncomfortable to exercise. There is no medical reason not to exercise during this time if you take care to wear proper clothing that prevents chafing and allows adequate ventilation.

Endometriosis. With endometriosis, portions of the inner lining of the uterus migrate outside the uterus. Endometriosis may or may not be accompanied by pain, which can usually be felt several days before the menstrual period and can occur at any time of the cycle. When severe, it may cause infertility.

When it comes to endometriosis, treatment varies from none at all for mild cases to anabolic steroids, which have a direct effect on exercise and numerous other side effects. Surgery or other medication may be recommended as well. Discuss all available treatments with your gynecologist so that you're fully informed about the risks and benefits. In most cases, you can continue to exercise during medical treatment.

The Plus Side of Exercise during Menopause

Finally, let's look at all those changes that occur a little later in life—during the Change, or menopause. Osteoporosis, heart disease, hot flushes, vaginal dryness, weight gain, depression—these are just a few of the classic symptoms of menopause. The good news for women who exercise is that the Change doesn't have to be such a negative experience.

Menopause is a woman's final menstrual period, which occurs when the ovaries have used up all functioning eggs. After menopause, estrogen levels fall drastically, which can speed up bone loss; this can be the most serious postmenopausal problem. Lower estrogen also contributes to vaginal dryness and hot flushes, symptoms that are not as serious but still can be quite uncomfortable.

The general benefits of exercise—like improved self-image and weight control—are a big plus during this time. Exercise provides specific relief as well. While it's not a cure-all for every change related to menopause, Dr. Shangold notes that exercise can help ward off osteoporosis, heart disease, weight gain and depression. And for the other symptoms, hormone-replacement therapy (a combination of estrogen and progesterone) can make a big difference.

Many active women question the need for hormone treatment after menopause. Health-conscious women often shy away from taking any medication, and because their exercise strengthens bones and helps fight heart disease, runners may feel their workouts will guard them against any menopausal problems. "These women tend to feel invincible and have an aversion to taking substances they consider unnatural," claims Dr. Shangold.

In April 1993, the Melpomene Institute and *Self* magazine conducted a survey of 332 women between the ages of 40 and 66 who exercise regularly and asked about their willingness to take hormone-replacement therapy. More than half the women were reluctant or had decided against it, while 35 percent were undecided. According to Melpomene's president Judy Mahle Lutter, "While figures vary, most studies suggest that only about 20 percent of all postmenopausal women are actually taking a form of hormone-replacement therapy."

As an alternative to hormone therapy, scientists are looking for a nutritional substitute. Soy protein with phytoestrogens is an exciting area of research.

It's been shown that, in some cases, estrogen therapy contributes to a higher risk of endometrial and breast cancers, but according to Dawn P. Lemcke, M.D., of the Virginia Mason Medical Center in Seattle, it is the only treatment shown to effectively maintain bone mass and cut down on fractures. Dr. Shangold agrees and believes the benefits of estrogen far outweigh any risks. She recommends both estrogen and exercise for postmenopausal women. In fact, the medical establishment supports hormone-replacement therapy almost 100 percent.

Strengthen Bones Early in Life

Along with estrogen, exercise is definitely your ally when it comes to keeping your bones strong. That's because as the muscles get stronger, they increase the stress on the bones during exercise, which stimulates bone growth. Thus, muscle building conditions your bones.

To head off osteoporosis, most doctors recommend exercise and adequate calcium intake, especially early in life, followed by hormone replacement during the first few years after menopause (unless certain risk factors rule a woman out). Osteoporosis, which literally means porous bones, is the root cause of most broken bones in older people. Women are eight times more likely to suffer from the disease than men because of hormonal differences. Women have less bone mass than men and lose it at a faster rate, especially after menopause.

To cut your risk of osteoporosis later in life, you need to start with strong bones early. Bone mass peaks between the ages of 25 and 40, the time when it is important to lay down a strong foundation of bone. This peak time for building bone is followed by a progressive loss of bone mass. Do athletes lose bone? As far as she knows, no one has done any long-term studies of bone mass in athletes, says Dr. Shangold, who adds, "but athletes probably lose bone, too."

Bone loss is not to be taken lightly. Researchers suggest that when bone is lost earlier in life, as it is in young amenorrheic women, it may not be completely reversible later. Body weight was found to be an important predictor of bone density as the menstrual cycle became more irregular.

According to Charlotte Sanborn, Ph.D., of Texas Women's University in Denton, missing periods and loss of bone mass are not only because of low body fat as has traditionally been thought. She says that too many women simply don't eat enough calories. "It could be that calorie-energy drain shuts down the system," said Dr. Sanborn at a meeting of the International Sport Nutrition Conference.

If menstruation starts again, it may boost bone mass—but only in very young runners. One study found that in a group of amenorrheic girl runners who regained their periods, bone mass increased in those 15 to 16 years old, while in those over 17, it did not. So as a rule, it's better to maintain your periods.

Kegel Exercises: Strengthening Your Bladder

It can dampen more than your spirits to find that in a brief moment of exertion—during a cough or a laugh, perhaps—your bladder leaks. If you leak while you run, the situation gets more worrisome. Stress urinary incontinence—involuntary urine leakage—occurs when your pelvic floor (the muscles around your bladder and uterus) is weak and abdominal pressure is suddenly increased. It can be aggravated by exercise like running. Running, however, doesn't cause a leaky bladder or make the condition worse, says Dr. Shangold.

Speaking at a conference on medical issues of active and athletic women, Kathe Wallace, a physical therapist at the Virginia Mason Medical Center, claimed that pelvic floor dysfunction is generally ignored. Yet, in a survey of women who exercise regularly, she noted that 47 percent reported some degree of incontinence during physical exertion.

A doctor can assess the muscle tone of your pelvic muscles during a routine pelvic exam. Wallace recommends women learn to perform Kegel exercises as a regular part of a fitness routine, in addition to the times of pregnancy and recovery from childbirth. Kegel exercises are designed to strengthen the pelvic muscles. Doing Kegels alternately contracts and relaxes the muscles around your vagina, and they are also helpful for improving bladder control.

To make sure you're working the proper muscles, you can place a finger just inside your vagina as though inserting a tampon. When you contract the muscles, you should feel the finger being squeezed.

You can also get a feel for where these muscles are and how to contract them by stopping or slowing the flow of urine without tensing the muscles of the buttocks, legs or abdomen. If you stop the flow, you are using the muscles we're talking about.

When performing Kegel exercises, you should also concentrate on relaxing the muscles in the surrounding area, says Wallace. Once you've perfected the technique, you can do Kegels anytime, anywhere. Work up to doing 25 at a time, squeezing for ten seconds each. You should start seeing improvement in urine control—and fewer "accidents"—after about two weeks.

CHAPTER 4

THE PREGNANT RUNNER

Two for the Road

Joan and her husband, Scott, have two children—a daughter, Abby, and a son, Anders—born three and five years after Joan's victory in the 1984 Olympic Marathon. Throughout both pregnancies, Joan continued to run as enthusiastically as ever. Here she shares her experiences and what she has learned from them.

I enjoy sharing the stories of how I ran through both my pregnancies with very few problems. Well-known runner and sports medicine expert Joan Ullyot, M.D., summed up my attitude best when she observed, "Gazelles run when they're pregnant. Why should it be any different for women?"

Running was just that natural for me. In fact, I often felt better running while pregnant than when I wasn't pregnant. I felt so fluid, so in control of my running, my diet and my lifestyle. Although I have always worked on creating balance among these elements, I was even more conscientious about them while I was pregnant. Everything seemed to mesh together for me during that time.

I can still recall several memorable runs during my pregnancies, and I'll never forget one special morning. It was a beautiful winter day—snowy but sunny—and I felt great running on snow-packed roads. I was as pregnant as possible—for that evening, I gave birth. I had gone out for a five-miler, but I felt I could have run forever. No matter how much time passes, I can still mentally put myself on that road. A perfect run on a perfect day.

Running with a New Partner

As always with exercise and my body, I was keenly aware of how my body reacted to running during pregnancy. As my ligaments loosened, I felt minor twinges from muscles being pulled and stretched. I noticed that as my belly swelled, my stride shortened. Fortunately,

KEEP THAT BABY COOL

Pregnant runners must take care not to overheat; an internal temperature above 101°F can cause birth defects in the developing fetus. Mona Shangold, M.D., noted author and sports medicine gynecologist at Hahnemann University Hospital in Philadelphia, recommends this approach: Determine your proper exertion level by taking your temperature rectally. An oral reading may not be accurate because hard breathing during running cools your mouth so that the reading is falsely low. So, immediately after finishing a run, head for a private spot and take a rectal reading. (You have about five minutes to get an accurate reading.)

Take your postexercise temperature in early pregnancy, suggests Dr. Shangold, to make sure you're "keeping your cool." If you exercise at the same approximate intensity with every run, you don't have to take your temperature every time. Should you pick up the pace or increase your distance, however, take your temperature again.

since weight usually increases gradually during pregnancy, I had time to adapt. And I didn't gain much—only 15 to 18 pounds each time. (By the way, this gain was normal for me, as I was very active and am a small person. Most women, though, gain 25 to 35 pounds during pregnancy.)

In my first trimester, my approach to running changed entirely, and I kept my training conservative. For the first time, I wasn't running only for myself but with someone else in mind. I made sure to follow the cardinal rules of not running to the point of breathlessness or getting overheated, so as not to endanger my baby's health.

On average, I ran about two-thirds of my normal mileage (which had been 80 to 100 miles per week), and my pace was at least a minute per mile slower than my previous comfortable pace. My longest runs were 12 to 13 miles, which I did about once a week. For some runners, this might seem too rigorous, but a 13-miler represented only about 60 percent of my usual long-distance run of 20 miles.

Occasionally, I did participate in a road race but not to compete. I paired up with a friend and ran at a pace where we could talk comfortably. I sometimes wonder how I would have done if I could have competed during pregnancy. I felt so good—physically and mentally—that it was hard to remember I was actually carrying a baby. Except for being careful not to push the pace, everything came so naturally.

To Each Her Own

Not all women runners will take the same approach to running during pregnancy. Nor should they. When it comes to pregnancy, each woman responds differently. I've known women who felt like I did—perfectly fine running through their entire pregnancies. I have also known women runners who, by choice or necessity or a physician's advice, didn't jog a step the entire time. Your decision must be based on your feelings, your doctor's advice and your individual condition.

When I describe my daily running schedule, some people shake their heads in disbelief. But it was right for me. If I had been asked to work in an office sitting at a desk from 9 to 5, I don't think I could have done it. Of course, other women do it all the time. It just goes to show that what we find comfortable depends on our routines and on our attitudes. In many cases, a woman can continue to run throughout her pregnancy, to her and her baby's benefit, as long as she follows the basic safety guidelines that are outlined in this chapter.

If you are committed to continuing your running, be sure to find a supportive obstetrician or midwife who will help you plan your exercise program. Although some doctors don't endorse running during pregnancy, most recognize the benefits of an exercise program during this time. Should a doctor tell you not to run for no apparent medical reason, feel free to seek a second opinion.

For athletically inclined women, being told not to exercise during pregnancy can be more stressful than the exercise itself. In the seventh month of my second pregnancy, I was ordered to stop running because of low amniotic fluid (the water that surrounds and protects the baby). I didn't run a step for four days until I saw a specialist in high-risk pregnancies (a perinatologist), who reassured me that everything appeared fine. For those four days out of my routine, though, I was so stressed that I'm sure my blood pressure rose.

Starting Out

What if you weren't a runner but catch the running bug after becoming pregnant? According to the American College of Obstetricians and Gynecologists, it is okay to begin exercising (like running) even if you didn't do it before you were pregnant. Doctors, however, aren't sure what a safe limit is, says Mona Shangold, M.D., noted author and sports medicine gynecologist at Hahnemann University Hospital in Philadelphia, so you have to go easy, even slower than a beginner, and watch your perceived level of exertion. "Be sure you don't get out of breath or start to feel like you're working too hard." Brisk walking or walking and intermittently breaking out into a run are ways to get started. Take extra care to avoid getting overheated.

Running during Pregnancy: How Joan Did It

Throughout both my pregnancies, I kept the following guidelines in mind, and they helped me adapt and enjoy my running safely. Many of these tips come from the Melpomene Institute for Women's Health

Research in St. Paul, a well-respected, nonprofit organization that does extensive research on women's health and physical activity.

Plan with a pro. Discuss your plans to exercise during pregnancy with your obstetrician or midwife (preferably one who is supportive and knowledgeable about exercise). Don't be timid about questioning your doctor. In your initial interview, ask about her attitude toward exercise and pregnancy. Many pregnant women—runners and nonrunners alike—shop around before choosing a doctor or midwife.

Be flexible. Don't have preset goals for exercising during pregnancy. Be willing to adapt over time as your body changes.

Train, don't strain. Pay strict attention to your perceived level of exertion and run more conservatively. Caution: No speed work or anaerobic running. That is, stay within your target heart rate zone. Limit sessions to 30 minutes.

Be cool: cool down. To slowly lower your heart rate back to normal, end your run with a walk. If you stop abruptly, blood tends to pool in your limbs, especially the legs.

Know when to quit. Stop your exercise if you begin cramping, gasping for breath or feeling dizzy. If you have pain, bleeding or your water breaks, get medical help immediately.

Try something less demanding. If, because of weight gain or stress and strain on your joints, running becomes uncomfortable, consider an alternative activity such as walking or swimming. Select an activity that does not introduce new stress but rather will make exercise easier for you. Swimming, for example, may be more enjoyable because the water helps support extra weight.

Choose the right time. When weather is extreme, run in the most temperate part of the day. In winter, the middle of the day is usually best. In summer, run early or toward evening, when the sun's rays are weaker.

Dress for success. Wear appropriate clothing to avoid overheating (see page 189). In warm weather, wear light, loose clothing. In winter, wear several layers so you can add or remove pieces as your body temperature changes. Don't wear tight-fitting clothes that might restrict circulation.

Seek support. During pregnancy, your breasts tend to swell, so find a comfortable, supportive bra. Some women find lightweight maternity girdles or support stockings give added support and comfort. Or try a unitard. When I was pregnant, I developed a hernia, so for extra support across my middle I wore a Lycra bathing suit while running.

Since you are carrying extra weight and may feel unbalanced during pregnancy, it's especially important to wear well-cushioned, stable running shoes. (See chapter 13 about choosing shoes.)

Drink for two. Be sure to drink plenty of fluids before and after you run, even if you have to urinate frequently.

Be kind to your back. During pregnancy, your lower back is under pressure from the extra weight pulling you forward. Pay attention to posture and balance so that your lower back doesn't sustain extra stress.

Be sensible. The usual safety caveats apply if you run during pregnancy. Run with others, if possible. Always let someone know when and where you're going. Take money in case you need to phone someone to pick you up. Carry your name, address, phone number and an emergency contact.

Go easy. Be sure to get adequate rest. Exercising to the point of exhaustion or chronic fatigue does neither mother nor baby any good and can be harmful.

Eat well. Needless to say, what you eat in the months before, during and after pregnancy is critical to your health and your baby's. (See chapter 12 for details on how to be sure you're getting enough iron, calcium and other essential nutrients.)

Resuming Training: Getting Back to Normal

Even if you've stayed fairly active, as I did, throughout your pregnancy, you need a little time to recover from childbirth. My babies were slightly lighter than average at birth: 5 pounds 12 ounces and 6 pounds 1 ounce. But this was expected as I am a small woman (5-foot-3, 105 pounds), and I was active during my pregnancies. After my babies were born, I returned fairly quickly to running and eventually worked up to my normal training levels.

After childbirth, I did a lot of walking in the first few weeks, working up to two miles per session. Eventually, I walked with the baby in a carrier pouch strapped across my chest and gradually increased the pace.

When I felt ready to begin running, I left the baby at home. You should never jog or run while carrying an infant; the shaking would be extremely dangerous to your child's developing organs, especially the brain. I walked until I felt the urge to break into a run, then slowly increased my running, working up to between three and ten miles a day. While I increased my total weekly mileage, I did not exceed ten miles at a time until six to eight weeks postpartum.

A word of caution: Despite how good you may feel after childbirth, don't resume running too soon. My first delivery was most difficult, and the prolonged strain of labor may have stressed my body more than expected. Afterward, I may have started training too quickly. Perhaps I did not give my lower back and pelvic ligaments a chance to return to their original function and position. In fact, this may have caused the slight misalignment in my hips that I have had ever since. After giving birth the second time, I waited a week before I started walking.

Since the birth of my children, I've had problems with my lower back and hips. Deb Merrill, my neuromuscular therapist who has gone through two pregnancies herself, believes that carrying more than 20 extra pounds while running over six miles a day can create imbalances in the hips and back. She also feels that returning to training too soon, while the body is still adjusting, may be harmful.

So, just how soon is too soon? It depends. Dr. Shangold says that after a normal vaginal delivery, you can most likely resume exercise when you have no pain, but wait at least two days before doing any aerobic exercise. Exercise begun sooner may increase bleeding and delay healing.

If you've had a cesarean section, you should probably take longer—doctors say you should give yourself at least one week before light exercise (at a comfortable, leisurely effort) and at least three weeks for intense exercise (close to all-out effort). Check with your physician to be sure what's right for you.

Dr. Shangold emphasizes that every woman is different. "No scientific studies have looked at this yet. Each case must be viewed individually." The one thing she stresses is, "Listen to your own body."

If swimming is in your exercise program, Dr. Shangold cautions you to wait until all vaginal bleeding and discharge have stopped, usually a few weeks after delivery. Water sports may lead to bacterial infection of the uterus, fallopian tubes or ovaries if you take the plunge before the cervix closes.

After my first baby was born, I swam at a nearby indoor pool. I would nurse Abby in the locker room until she was sleepy. Then I would put her in a car seat a safe distance away from the pool at the end of the lane in which I trained, so I could see her after every lap. I asked the lifeguards to keep an eye on her and to call me if she fussed, but they never had to. They were well-prepared. At my pool, they had seen their share of mothers and babies doing the same thing.

You have everything to gain and nothing to lose by taking a low-key approach to training during and after pregnancy. My advice is to try power walking, swimming and other low-impact exercises. Dr. Shangold agrees: "Hold back until you feel more than ready to resume training."

Postpartum Do's

Dr. Shangold advises women runners to keep these general guidelines in mind as they renew their workouts after giving birth.

- If you had a tear or cut (episiotomy) during childbirth, wait until all soreness is gone before you exercise vigorously.

- If you begin to bleed heavily during exercise, stop and give yourself more time to recover—probably a few days until the bleeding diminishes.

- Include a careful warm-up and cool-down with your exercise. Walk or run at a slow pace for five to ten minutes.

- Work on regaining your muscle tone. Perform Kegel exercises (see page 30) to tone the pelvic floor (the muscles around the vagina and bladder) as soon as it is comfortable. After a vaginal delivery, you can also start working on abdominal muscles while still in bed by lifting your head from the pillow. Do not do this if you've had a cesarean.

• If you are breast-feeding your newborn, drink plenty of fluids and wear a good nursing bra.

• To avoid discomfort from engorgement (when breasts are filled with milk), some women breast-feed just before exercising, but you may breast-feed at any time. Despite claims that breast milk contains higher concentrations of lactic acid after exercise, giving the milk an unpleasant taste, Dr. Shangold contends there is very little evidence of this effect. (Lactic acid is a by-product of muscle metabolism, created during intense exercise.)

• Take it easy on yourself. Don't push yourself into your old routine too quickly. Fatigue is a common problem; if you're tired, consider a nap rather than exercise.

CHAPTER 5

RUNNING AT ANY AGE

What Women Need to Know

From the time I was 11 years old, I loved to run," says Joan. "When I ran, my enjoyment and excitement came naturally." Such are Joan's memories of running as a young girl—positive memories that turned a joyful childhood activity into a lifelong career. It's no wonder she concludes, "At any level and at any age, I think running is the path to both physical health and a healthy attitude."

As a girl, Joan loved childhood games that involved running as much as running for its own sake. That carried over into team and individual sports. "I played kickball and baseball with the boys in the neighborhood, competed at basketball, field hockey and tennis in high school and skied since I was four. And looking back, I've channeled part of each sport into my running career."

A Running Start

Children love to run; for most, it comes naturally. That's how Joan believes it should be. While she's enthusiastic about girls running, she is careful to qualify that enthusiasm. "When I was little, girls weren't given much opportunity or encouragement to run. Now I'm the mother of a young daughter who has shown some interest. While I'm glad she's active, I'm careful not to push her. I'm very sensitive to how parents can try to live vicariously through their children, however unintentional.

"It's fine to encourage and support children if they show interest," says Joan. She feels the flood of children's races is great if they are low-key events "with friends and maybe a Popsicle or a ribbon for everyone at the end." She recommends, however, that parents of young children run with them (which she does with hers) but keep pace just behind them. That way, they don't inadvertently push their children's pace.

"The best thing we can teach our children is how to play and to play well. We should give them as many opportunities as possible and introduce them to a variety of disciplines. By the time they're in high school, they can begin to hone in on the activities that most interest them."

Like Mother, Like Children

Running moms are great role models for both boys and girls. But Joan feels that it's especially important to imbue girls with a love of and interest in sports. Boys are automatically encouraged, often at home and at school, to be involved and to enjoy sports. Girls need the same kind of attention. When Joan goes out to run, she often invites her daughter, Abby, to ride along on her bicycle.

Perhaps the best way to cultivate an interest and ability in sports is simply to share your own love for it. Co-author Gloria Averbuch, mother of two daughters, offers some useful suggestions.

Share the fun. Let your children know you enjoy running. Invite them to join in or do what they like to do—skipping, jumping and so forth. Perhaps they can join you as you warm up or cool down. Or you can take walks or go hiking together.

Keep going year-round. During bad weather, try indoor fitness—

jumping hurdles made of pillows and blankets, skipping rope, running in place, running obstacle courses and the like. If it's too hot to run, go swimming.

Sign up for family fun runs or walks. Many adult races have short distance races for youngsters. Encourage other family members to attend and cheer the children on. Celebrate afterward with a picnic or special outing.

Throw a party. Plan running- or sports-related theme birthday parties. Ice skating and swimming parties are always popular. Gloria and her family have created parties based on relay races and hiking, for example. Children enjoy being part of this creative process—let them choose their favorite party sport. You may notice an added plus is that your party guests are much more ready for orderly sitting activities (for games or birthday cake) after physical activity.

Set a new course. Mapping out different routes in the neighborhood can add some variety and interest to a run. If your children want you to, time them as they run a particular route. Like measurements on a growth chart, children enjoy seeing their progress and improvement.

Give P.E. credit. Show as much interest in physical education class as academic subjects. Try to get involved in school programs by assisting with class or after-school activities.

Bring along siblings. Include younger children in fitness activities, too. While one child runs up and back, for example, the younger one can cover half the distance or run a shorter loop.

Pre-teen Years: The Building Blocks of Training

"Running is a great lifelong sport," says John Babington, coach at the Liberty Athletic Club for 19 years and assistant coach for the 1996 Olympic women's track-and-field team, "and the goal of the pre-teen runner should be to look toward pushing to excel when she is older." Babington's philosophy on training for young girls has taken shape during his 19 years of experience with the many young runners he has coached at the Liberty Athletic Club, a renowned running club that serves the New England area.

At this age, Babington emphasizes, running should be fun. But he maintains that growing girls also need to learn the basics—how to warm up and cool down, how to pace themselves and how to stretch. Running should be part of a general introduction and appreciation of sports and fitness rather than part of an earnest training program for competition. As he puts it, "They should be training to learn how to train."

The best way to achieve this goal, he says, is to introduce competition gradually. "Formal competitive experience is an option, not a necessity."

Several young runners who were coached by Babington have achieved great success. And they all followed his program of basics first. Darlene Beckford, a 1500-meter runner and Harvard University all-American, Olympic medalist Lynn Jennings and Joan didn't compete on a high level before age 14.

"I don't believe in striving for extremely fast times and intense levels of competition," states Babington on training the young runner. "I have witnessed the demise of an entire generation of hotshots—some running sub-five-minute miles before completing high school and as full of promise as Joan Samuelson. But just about every one of them never reached the elite level as an adult." He says the main reason was serious motivational problems and burnout, which resulted in these athletes dropping out of the sport.

Finding a Mentor

When a child is interested in running or other sports, many parents eventually consider the question of whether to work with a coach. Joan contends that this issue is best resolved by the child herself.

In some cases, a helpful teacher or coach may suggest that a girl come out for practice or try out for a team. For a reticent youngster, this can be just the encouragement she needs.

Sometimes, a young girl or woman (pre-college) will take the initiative and approach a coach on her own, or perhaps with her parents. This takes a fair amount of confidence, but there's less chance that she will be pushed into something she isn't keen about.

In Joan's case, she knew her goals and was highly motivated. She recognized when the right person came along. "I met John Babington when I was in high school. He struck me as a good coach, someone I wanted to impress. I was comfortable enough to make my own introduction. I was the one who wanted to test myself in big track meets."

So, above all, make sure the initiative, and the choice to be coached, truly comes from the child.

Wanted: Wise Parents

"The best parent of a young runner is supportive and approving," says Babington, "but leaves the logistics of training and racing to others." He notes that the parents of Jennings, Beckford and Samuelson, while applauding their daughters' efforts and accomplishments, did not get bogged down in the details of training schedules and racing plans. It is always best, he feels, for a girl who is serious about her running to have an experienced coach or mentor. This should be someone other than a parent, to keep those roles separate.

The Challenge of Puberty

"From ages 9 through 12, girls are perpetual-motion machines," says Babington. "Physically and psychologically, running is effortless for them."

But one of the biggest crises for young girl runners involves the physical and psychological changes related to puberty—the shift from childhood to maturity. Once a girl navigates this often tough transition, Babington points out, better times can be ahead. That's because the increased physical capabilities of an adult allow for higher levels of effort, and thus, of performance.

Of the young runners he has worked with who have achieved a high level of success, says Babington, all had gone through puberty before competing seriously.

Run Right, Eat Right

Instilling the basics of good health is just as vital as learning the basics of training. And healthful eating habits are crucial for young girls. According to Mona Shangold, M.D., noted author and sports medicine gynecologist at Hahnemann University Hospital in Philadelphia, young girls (under the age of 20) are more likely to develop eating disorders, ranging from malnutrition to anorexia. Based on her experiences with her peers as a young runner, Joan believes the problem is quite extensive, and she emphasizes the need for focusing on it and moving away from the idealized lean stereotype. "I think coaches are among the first to see signs of eating disorders in athletes, so they are in a position to seek professional help for their students."

Poor nutrition at this age can lead to amenorrhea (absence of menstruation). These girls are more susceptible to menstrual irregularity, says Dr. Shangold, because their reproductive systems have not matured. "In order for menstruation to occur, the brain requires a delicate balance of carefully timed events," she says. Any girl who has not begun to menstruate by age 16 should be examined by a doctor, although she can continue exercising, she adds.

Bones grow at a phenomenal rate during puberty, says Dr. Shangold. Failing to menstruate suggests low levels of estrogen, which, along with poor nutrition, could prevent proper bone growth. The combination of amenorrhea, reduced bone density and disordered eating in young women involved in intense training has been termed the *female athlete triad* by Kimberly L. Yeager, M.D., assistant director of Public Health Practice at San Diego State University, and the long-range consequences could be serious. (See page 25.)

Women over 40: It's Never Too Late to Go for It

Running truly is lifelong. And more women over 40 are taking up running or continuing to run into their fifties and beyond. The benefits? Increased strength, agility, stamina and energy, stronger bones, lesser risk of heart disease, improved weight control and a terrific sense of well-being. No wonder that, with an estimated 13 million women runners in this country today, the fastest growing group is women over 40.

Look for Joan Samuelson to be on the roads indefinitely. "I'll never retire," proclaims Joan. "I'll always want to see how I stack up against my personal best times and compare myself with both my age group and the up-and-coming stars. Of course, the focus and level of competition will not always be at the same level that it's been in the past."

She points out that the great thing about running is that even if you put it "on the shelf" for a while, it's always there. "Running is like riding a bicycle—you never forget. The bike may get rusty from lack of use, but it just needs a little oil and some air in the tires to run smoothly again."

Masters Running: Learning from Leaders in Women's Running

Once you turn 40, you're in a whole new running class: the masters. As Joan sees it, "Masters running calls for an entirely new set of goals. I'm not there yet, but I'm already beginning to think about running as a master. It opens up a whole new world.

"I think part of the challenge of being a master is taking your lifestyle into consideration and deciding on new goals because you're in a different time in your life."

Joan considers possible changes in her training and racing goals. "I certainly haven't run a 10-K time I've been excited about in the last few years. Maybe I'll focus on that. Or maybe I'll feel that I don't have a lot of speed left in my legs, and I'll stick to running longer, like the marathon, which has always come relatively easily to me. I do think I'll have to concentrate on one or the other. I don't think you can do it all as a master. It's hard to mix endurance and speed.

"On the other hand, some masters enjoy new freedoms. They're starting fresh. Women over 50 may have an entirely different perspective. Maybe they are facing the empty nest. They often don't have the day-to-day responsibilities of mothering. Running can be a great socializing tool and a way for women to develop unrealized potential. They may want to get a coach, push hard, go for it. I think that's great," says Joan.

Women in this age range can be greatly inspired and encouraged by masters runners whose accomplishments are outstanding for an athlete at any age. Such an example is Priscilla Welch of Great Britain, who was sixth in the 1984 Los Angeles Olympic Marathon and won the New York City Marathon—*after* turning 40.

Another inspiring master is Francie Larrieu Smith, who has not only the longest but the most versatile career of any top distance runner, woman or man. She has made five Olympic teams and two World Championship teams for distances from 800 meters to the marathon. At 39, she qualified for the Olympics in Barcelona, a feat that inspires Joan in her Olympic quest for 1996, when she'll be 39. Between the ages of 16 and 38, she held 17 American outdoor track records. In her masters career, she has already set an American record for the 10-K on the roads.

How has her running changed with age? Larrieu Smith says it is difficult for her to judge objectively the effects of aging on her running, since her career has changed so much over the years. In her twenties and early thirties, she was training for shorter track races. "That's much easier than marathon training." So, she asks, are the effects of wear and tear from aging or is it marathon training? Larrieu Smith suspects it may be the long-distance running. But she points out, as Joan does, "There are other reasons, besides training, why things change; life intervenes." But the basic ingredient is still the same: "I love to run."

Does Aging Slow Us Down?

We know that exercise slows aging in women. But how does aging affect exercise? Michael Sargent, M.D., team physician at the University of Vermont in Burlington and a masters competitor, points out that although healing—both from strenuous exercise and injury—is slower as we age, the rate of recovery depends on the individual and her activity level. "Your muscle fibers do lose elasticity, and it is easier to get injured." But he says this doesn't necessarily mean you have to cut back.

While there is no reason to change the basic approach to training and fitness, there are some important medical implications for the beginning exerciser. According to Dr. Shangold, for those over 40 beginning an exercise program, a complete physical exam is universally recommended. Primarily, this checkup is to rule out the possibility of undetected heart disease.

Making a Fresh Start

Motivation—setting fresh and inspiring goals—is the key to running at any age. After 40, however, there are changes and adaptations that occur over time—whether because of the aging process or merely because of many years on the road.

Larrieu Smith offers some useful tips for running after 40.

Allow more recovery time. As many masters runners and coaches will tell you, a little more recovery time goes a long way toward keeping you fresh. After a hard training day, Larrieu Smith tends to take two easy days instead of only one (her former practice). In her case, she points out, "The work load hasn't lessened; it's just a different training cycle." Experiment to find what best serves you in balancing rest and recovery—whether it's amount, timing or both.

Listen to your body and heed its signals. "I know what it feels like when I'm running great," Larrieu Smith says. "And when I'm off, I want to know why. I'm open to all avenues of help—conventional . . . medical treatment as well as alternatives such as chiropractic treatment and acupuncture."

Pamper yourself. Since 1982, Larrieu Smith has been getting regular massages. "If for nothing else, it's great at least once a month to relieve stress." Perhaps there are other treats—new clothes, a night out—that offer you special rewards.

Take a more relaxed attitude. Ease up on controlling your body. It's a fact that the body does change at various stages of life. If you want to enjoy your exercise, you have to practice self-acceptance. "I've given into weighing a little more," says Larrieu Smith, who has gone up five pounds since turning 40. Basically, she concludes, "I'm not willing to starve myself."

Build strength. In order to maintain muscular strength, which can decline with age in both women and men, Larrieu Smith includes strength training drills. (See page 148 for more details on strength training.)

Remember the basics. That's what Larrieu Smith did in her 41st year. After a period of overracing in her first year as a master, she returned to what has always worked best for her: a methodical, structured approach including strength training, base mileage, hill training and selective racing. Now she says, "I don't race unless I'm ready."

Set specific goals. Concrete goals are important no matter what your level—even without racing. Particularly, as she puts it, because "life intervenes." Her advice: "If you want to race and get the best possible results, choose races carefully and focus on them."

Clearly, one's outlook continues to be a major factor in motivation. Concludes Larrieu Smith, "In my mind, I'm still young. When I go to the starting line, I still perceive myself as racing in the open division. But it's nice to be 40—at least I usually win my age group!"

Her goal? To make yet another Olympic team in the marathon. More important, her overall aim has never changed: "Do the best I possibly can."

PART II

RUNNING FASTER AND STRONGER

CHAPTER 6

TRAINING TO BE YOUR BEST

Perfecting the Art of Running

Beyond simply logging miles, training is a delicate balance of physical and mental effort. In this chapter, Joan reveals what she has learned through her coaches and her coaching as well as from years of experience, including her unique personal training tips.

Running just to run—at an easy and comfortable pace—is fine if it meets your needs and goals. But running to train goes further. When you train, you push yourself to improve and to meet specific goals.

Are you a beginner? Your goal may be to run a certain distance (two miles) or for a certain amount of time (20 minutes). As an intermediate runner, you may put in 30 minutes every day you run but at different speeds or over a variety of terrains. And once you've raced, you may be aiming to improve your personal record or even break someone else's record.

Even if you're not planning to race, though, you can train to improve your general fitness level and add interest and variety to your workouts.

And don't forget your potential as an athlete. You'll never know how good you can get until you try.

As those in the know will tell you—and like the coaches and physiologists stress throughout this book—it's consistency over years of training that makes great athletes. You can continue to develop and evolve and fulfill your potential by applying the same commitment and training principles as the elite.

Longevity and, particularly, improvement take effort. Achieving your maximum potential requires an understanding of training and also learning to analyze your own personal cycles and plateaus, motivation and goals.

Running Partners

How do you like your running: alone, with a friend or in a group? I usually run alone. Twice a week, however, I have company, which, in addition to the social aspect, serves a specific training purpose. Once a week, I run with a woman friend who is considerably slower than me but not so slow as to make the pace uncomfortable. This is my rest day, and the 7:30-a-mile pace we run forces me not to push too hard. What's more, we enjoy each other's company.

Running in a group serves the opposite purpose of helping me to push myself. I run with a group of men whose times for the marathon are between 2:18 and 3:00. They are local runners, most of whom I have met at road races or through friends. We do track workouts or hard road runs together. Based on ability and race schedules, we split up into groups and get each other through the workout. We have some great conversations, too, trading training tips, discussing techniques, rehashing the last race, planning the next one and covering family concerns and life in general.

Ideally, when picking a running partner, look for someone whose abilities are compatible with your goals. Maybe just a companion who keeps your pace steady or, as in my case, partners who help by pulling you into their pace. Just be careful not to get caught up in a pace that's too fast.

Track running can be a particularly inspiring and convenient way to share training because you can circle in a variety of ways that allow you to maintain constant contact. When two people run at different speeds, for example, the faster runner can take an outside track, while the slower one laps in the inside lane.

In the early 1980s, I ran some great track workouts with Olympic medalist Lynn Jennings and Judi St. Hilaire. Not only was it special having female company, I found it very motivational to be running relatively easily with two of the world's best runners.

Keeping Track of Your Progress

Most experts recommend keeping a running diary or log. I've used my own log to plan future training programs as well as to prepare for races. You can record your entries in a number of specially designed running diaries or your own homemade version.

In addition to keeping track of your training, use your diary to record your physical as well as emotional reactions to your running. Week-by-week, month-by-month or year-by-year comparisons are all useful. Don't hesitate to add details beyond a measure of mileage. How did you feel after your last long run? After double workouts? How is your running affected by your period, your diet or a hard race? Does the time of day affect your running? Those bits of information can tell you a lot about the effect of your lifestyle on your running, and vice versa.

Set Your Course: Using Training Loops

In terms of your running, a road is just a road—right? Not so. To make your training more effective and interesting, take some time to analyze the different features of your training loops—the courses you run.

My training loops around my home in Freeport, Maine, are like old, familiar friends. I've been running on them since 1983. I use them to both build and measure my fitness and as a form of mental therapy. I often do my best thinking and problem solving on these routes. As I run, I can prioritize important events of the day. I vary my loops and the intensity of my running based on my racing schedule and my own personal rhythms. Using different types of courses, or loops, in your training has several advantages.

First of all, it's nice to have a marker—a start and finish distance you can use as a gauge. Because I live on a peninsula, the first and the last mile of all my runs is always the same. I use it to warm up on the way out and to cool down on the way in. Beyond that, my favorite stretch includes an additional dirt road, making the distance 1½ miles. I use this section as a measure of my fitness. If I can run this stretch in under ten minutes, I'm really moving. If I go under nine minutes, I'm flying and know I'm capable of running fast races.

My loops also have optional subloops that I can run or not, depending on how I feel. Although I rarely vary my daily workouts, these optional training loops allow me to run according to how I truly feel—something you can't always assess until you've actually hit the road.

Many runners like to know the exact distance of their training loops, but I haven't technically measured all of mine. Sometimes I prefer to guess the distance, and, in fact, I intentionally assess them a bit short rather than risk estimating them too long. This way I'm sure I'm not "cheating" or assuming I've run a faster pace than I did. Also, it's one of my mental games to force myself to run longer and faster. I know, for example, that if I do a six-mile loop in under 38 minutes, I'm in good shape. If it turns out that, in fact, it's longer, then that's all for the better. I find that out when I run a good time on the track or in a race.

As my training partners know, I never take shortcuts. I always purposely run the turns wide. This can add a certain amount of distance to the run—as much as a quarter of a mile. In races, I always cut in on the tangents, of course, running the shortest possible distance. As a test of my willpower, I also add more distance to my loop, up to two miles, especially in preparation for a big race. Then I try to cover the total distance in the same time or even faster than I did without the addition. This system is a great way to test your fitness and to push yourself. It also gives you a discipline edge. By choosing to add distance and speed up the pace, you know you are ready and willing to work hard.

Keep in mind your own personal needs when laying out your training routes. Do you want a course with hills? Can you include a park with a drinking fountain? And you might want a variety of running surfaces. Be careful to balance out running on crowned roads by changing courses or directions, and try some dirt shoulders or soft paths to lessen impact. For safety as well as variety, I recommend creating several loops so your patterns don't become too predictable.

Most of my loops are tree-lined or surrounded by fields, but, for a change of scenery, I have a 12-mile route that takes me to downtown Freeport and back. I sometimes choose one route over others in order to avoid pollution, heavy pollen, busy traffic or construction. Running after dark requires paths without potholes or unlit spots.

Track Time

In the running world, there's a well-worn expression that says the track doesn't lie. It's a precise and universal 400-meter (440 yards, or ¼ mile) oval that guarantees the most accurate test of your fitness. Both physically and psychologically, track workouts are the hardest. But because there's a purity about running on the track, nothing is more exhilarating. In fact, I often feel higher emotionally after a track workout than after running 20 miles on roads.

Like many runners, I prefer to do my track workouts in the late afternoon or evening, when I tend to feel warmer and looser. Still, I usually do an easy morning run. I need to move around at some point during the day before a track workout. You may prefer to do the Stairmaster, stretch or take a power walk. Since I'm used to running in the mornings, if I wait until my afternoon workout, I sometimes feel sluggish by that time. In addition, it's always nice to know I have some training under my belt in case something prevents me from getting to the track.

The track is ideal for interval training, which is a sure way to improve your speed as well as endurance. In running intervals you're actually running repetitions (repeats, or reps) at various distances like 400 meters or speeds like a 5-K or mile race pace, then recovering (jogging slowly for a distance or a time) during the interval. Repeat each set (repetition and interval) until you've reached your limit without becoming totally exhausted.

You don't have to have a track for optimal interval training. Instead, you might mark off a distance (like a mile) with your car, or estimate a distance by using poles and fire hydrants along the road as markers. In a city, measure a typical block length (usually 80 to 130 meters) and run distances and intervals based on these multiples. For years, I avoided track workouts because the tight turns aggravated my leg-length discrepancy. During this time, I marked the distances on roads, trails, parking lots or fields.

Whether I'm on the track or not, if I'm doing any hard running, I greatly appreciate a training partner. In fact, it's almost impossible for me to do interval workouts alone. Even when it is possible, it's never as good. My workouts are usually of a much higher quality and more satisfying with at least one partner. If I don't have a running partner, sometimes I'll recruit someone at the track to run the last couple of laps of each mile repetition with me.

For most runners, track workouts are done in cycles. In the first part of my season, I use the track to test my level of fitness after coming off low-key training periods. I build on these initial track sessions right through to the big competitions or competitive season.

I begin on the track about three months before a serious marathon or other long-distance race. I start with longer segments like a mile each—running them at my marathon pace and slowly increasing in speed.

Usually, I warm up, cool down and run recovery laps in the opposite direction of my interval work. By doing this, I avoid putting disproportional physical stress on the same side of my body. On more deserted tracks, some runners even alternate directions with each interval.

In interval training, runners often find the first couple of repetitions are slower and more difficult. Once you're in the groove, though, you'll be able to find a power, ease and efficiency—almost like being on automatic pilot. When running any interval, work but don't fight. The key is to stay relaxed and to maintain good form. Make sure your elbows swing close to the body and your feet stay in a straight line; don't tense your shoulders or your face during the effort. Good form is important for running efficiency and injury prevention. You can even have your partner critique your form.

When I run on an indoor track, I do most of my workouts in the outside lane, where the torque of the turn is not as severe. I also like the fact that in the outside lane, there are fewer laps to the mile; it makes the workout seem shorter. There are usually eight laps (200 meters per lap) to a mile on an indoor track. If you're unsure of the measures, ask another runner or the attendant on duty at your facility.

Road Run Challenges

When you're in a group, try a tempo or fartlek run. A tempo run simulates race pace. Fartlek is a Swedish term meaning speed play—reps and intervals of various distances. Here are a couple of workouts that I like.

Single file. While running single file with four to six people, the back runner moves up—at any pace she desires—to the front. She may take the lead with a surge that the others must match or steadily increase the pace. After a designated time, the new last runner does the same.

This drill can be very valuable for simulating a race, as it involves changing gears, surging and running in a pack. You can practice when to make a move or to pick up the pace in an effort to pass your competition. These surges can also teach you patience when it comes to holding back at certain parts of the race in order to save something for later. My group does this single file run over at least two miles. It's also a good way to pick up the pace and work on leg speed at the end of a moderately long run like the last mile of an eight-miler.

Telephone pole training. Warm up by running comfortably for a mile or two. Using telephone poles or other regular markers, fashion a fartlek run. Start by picking up the pace for two or three markers. Recover with easy running. Pick up the pace for one more telephone pole. Do this as you feel—that's what fartlek is all about. The cooldown is similar to the warm-up.

Step counting. One of my favorite workouts is one I learned from coach Jack Daniels, Ph.D., noted exercise physiologist and head cross-country and track coach for men and women at the State University of New York at Cortland. Warm up by running an easy pace, then run sets of hard/easy intervals, starting at 10 paces for each. Next, run 20, 30 and so on until you reach 100 paces for each interval. Then count back down to 10 paces.

Training Tricks

I use some tricks in training to get me moving. I have six loops over which I have measured target times at certain check points. I try to challenge myself to hit those times. This gets me particularly motivated for an upcoming race. By the way, not every run needs to be a challenge. If I'm tired or I don't want a test, I don't time every run. Sometimes I simply leave my watch at home.

When I run in populated areas like along the Charles River in Boston or in Central Park in New York City, I try to run a pace at which no one can pass me. I feel that I train on a level not matched by many people. If someone passes me, I surge to catch up.

Often, when I'm running alone and I want to do some pick-ups or speed work, I accelerate my pace when I hear a car behind me and try to beat it to a certain landmark—a telephone pole, for example. This is an especially good game to play when you want to vary your intervals.

The ABCs of Workouts

My favorite workouts cover a variety of courses on tracks, roads and hills. In addition to the solid basics they provide, I often associate them with specific times in my life and career. Along with their training value, I try to build in a sense of fun and variety. You can try the following drills as they are, adapt them or use them as a basis to create your own.

Repeat miles. Do three to five per session, depending on your fitness; rest or jog slowly for a half-mile between each mile.

For me, repeat miles are part of my initial track workout in the beginning of a season or cycle, and they serve as a baseline for my conditioning. I know that if I can do five repeat miles (with a two-minute rest in between) at a 5:30 pace each, then my base conditioning is still intact. I can feel what's strong (my cardiovascular system, for example) and what isn't. Usually after this initial session, my legs feel rubbery. Then I know I have to work on my leg speed.

I routinely do three to five repeat miles per session, once a week. For beginners and even intermediates, however, one to three repeat miles will suffice. I increase the pace by 5 to 10 seconds per interval per week. Shorten your time accordingly: With a seven-minute repeat mile, you may be able to cut 10 to 15 seconds. It depends on how close you are to your best shape. You can also run shorter segments, like quarter-miles (400 meters), with rest intervals of about 100 meters. Run more of these—up to 10 to 12 times.

Ladders. So called because they go up and down in distance, ladders can add variety to interval training. Although some runners like to start with the shorter distance first, I've always preferred to start longer.

You can make these workouts even more challenging by progressively shortening the recovery jog—but take it easy if you're a beginner. Start with the one below.

BEGINNER'S LADDER

Fast run	*Recovery (jog/walk)*
400 meters (¼ mile)	200 meters (220 yards)
800 meters (½ mile)	400 meters (¼ mile)
1200 meters (¾ mile)	600 meters (660 yards)
800 meters (½ mile)	400 meters (¼ mile)
400 meters (¼ mile)	200 meters (220 yards)

EASY TEST

This ladder is a good test for fitness. Recovery time stays short, anywhere from 200 to 400 meters (220 yards to ¼ mile).

400 meters (¼ mile)

800 meters (½ mile)

1200 meters (¾ mile)

1600 meters (1 mile)

1200 meters (¾ mile)

800 meters (½ mile)

400 meters (¼ mile)

RUSSIAN LADDER

Based on a Russian training technique, this practice is meant to develop a kick.

Fast run	Recovery (jog)
400 meters (¼ mile)	200 meters (220 yards)
300 meters (330 yards)	150 meters (165 yards)
200 meters (220 yards)	100 meters (110 yards)
100 meters (110 yards)	400 meters (¼ mile)

Repeat the set.

JOAN'S LADDER

A truly tough test, this workout is often prescribed for competitive athletes.

Fast run	Recovery (jog)
1600 meters (1 mile)	800 meters (½ mile)
1200 meters (¾ mile)	600 meters (660 yards)
800 meters (½ mile)	400 meters (¼ mile)
400 meters (¼ mile)	400 meters (¼ mile)
800 meters (½ mile)	400 meters (¼ mile)
1200 meters (¾ mile)	600 meters (660 yards)

1-mile cool-down

Hill workouts. To develop leg strength and improve cardiovascular fitness, I do hill workouts. Running hills not only develops this specialized strength, it alleviates the impact of hard running on flat surfaces. There are several ways I do these workouts.

Hilly loops. When I do a hilly loop, I choose a route that suits my distance, usually six to ten miles, with hills at varying intervals. You can shorten the total distance if you're a beginner—or just run fewer or shorter hills. Every time I approach a hill on the loop, I pick up the pace while concentrating on my form and stride length. I especially focus on using my arms to help me get up the hill. I pump them in a strong and rhythmic fashion and keep them bent at right angles. To be truly energy-efficient, I shorten my stride on the ascent and lengthen my stride while leaning forward on the descent.

Hill repeats. Depending on whether I'm trying to develop my speed or my strength and endurance, I choose either a short, steep hill, which takes me about 30 seconds to run, or a long, gradual hill that takes one to two minutes to ascend. Often, my longer hills have a short plateau after which the hill rises a second time. When I get to the top of these hills, I turn around, jog to the bottom and start again. I do five to ten repeats. Choose fewer repeats if you are a beginner or are just beginning hill workouts in your training cycle.

Out-and-back runs. For this workout, choose a hilly route and pick up the pace on the hills. Then reverse, continuing to pick up the pace on the hills on the way back.

My out-and-back run carries me over a three-mile stretch containing six hills of various sizes. I run each of them hard, turn around at the end of the three miles and head back, working the hills in the opposite direction. For beginners, cut back on the number of hills or don't run hard for all of them.

Many runners drive, bicycle or jog to a specific hill for a workout. If you have the "perfect" hill, it's worth the effort to get to it in the same way you make the effort to get to a track. I know many coaches and athletes who travel to sand dunes for hill workouts. The sand provides significant resistance and is a particularly challenging and effective way to develop strength.

Testing Your Speed

After two months of longer track workouts, I'm usually ready to ease up on both training volume and intensity as I begin to taper for an upcoming marathon or competitive road-racing schedule. I shorten the intervals to achieve sharpness.

Sharpening Intervals: 400 meters (¼ mile), 200 meter (220 yard) recovery; repeat the sequence five or six times.

Beginner's Version: 400 meters (¼ mile), 200 meter (220 yard) recovery (jog or walk); repeat the sequence three or four times.

For my sharpening intervals, I might do quarter-mile repeats beginning at 75 seconds and finishing in 68 or 69 seconds. Saving strength to finish the intervals faster is more exhilarating and satisfying for me than finishing with slower intervals. This is good both physically and psychologically, because it prepares me for the best-case race scenario, in which I finish strong.

Particularly when you're tapering, it's always a good sign when you have completed a workout exactly as you set out to do, yet feeling that you have enough energy and strength left over to do just one more. Don't. Finishing a workout with something left over is best. Too many runners leave their best racing on the track or roads when they push too hard in pre-race workouts.

When You're "On"—Or Not

Use your training to build your confidence. Certain occasions and signs will tell you when you are "on." Notice the subtle clues, not just the obvious indicators of time and distance. I still vividly recall my last 20-mile training run before the Los Angeles Olympics, for example. A couple of guys were painting a house along the way, and one of them called out to me, "You're flying!" I knew it; I felt it—and the confidence that goes with it—but it was reinforced by someone else who could see it, too.

But training is not always "on." Your peak times usually seem to balance out with times when you feel sluggish. Accept these "down" times. Don't attempt the same training and don't compare. If necessary, take new routes or leave your watch at home.

I have a flat period a couple of times a year, when I'm relatively low-key in my training and racing. At these times, I'm not as concerned with my weekly mileage or my pace. I don't go to the track, and I'm more casual about my running—willing to fit it in during the day whenever I can. Usually, these spells come after the spring and fall, when I've just run a marathon. In May and June, I'm usually recovering from the Boston Marathon and am content to spend a lot of time and energy working in my garden. In my winter down cycle, I concentrate on projects around the house and skiing (both cross-country and downhill) with my family.

I've learned not to push too hard during these rest cycles. But for many runners—and I've been one of them—this is easier said than done. We so often want to keep working hard and making progress. But it can take just as much discipline to rest as to train hard. Remember, rest is an equal part of the training equation. My older brother, who is a doctor, often reminds me that rest is the basis of all activity.

Signs of Overtraining

Speaking of rest, this is a good place to talk about overtraining, when you just seem to go stale and lose your ambition and motivation. To avoid falling into the trap of overtraining remember that a cycle of stress and rest is how your body best absorbs the effects of your training. So this may be the time for rest or some alternative exercise.

You can avoid overdoing it if you follow the standard rule of thumb: Increase your training by no more than 10 percent per week. But while it is a good general rule, I have always believed the best way to learn your limits is by experience. For myself, I can run hard for a couple of consecutive sessions, but then I need to take it easy for at least two days—rather than follow the one-day-hard/one-day-easy rule. I have learned by experience how to gauge overtraining.

Watch for the signs that you've overdone it: feeling flat in training, lack of appetite, insomnia, general apathy or crankiness. Also, when you suspect overtraining, study your running diary and review your lifestyle over the past few weeks.

Coaching—Do You Need Help?

To be coached or not to be coached? For many women who become serious about running, seeking coaching is ultimately a question. Runners who have begun racing and wish to improve further might benefit by seeking coaching advice. Another case for coaching is the runner who has been steadily improving and then becomes stalled.

A good coach can motivate you and help you decide when you are on the right path or when you might need extra rest. She can also suggest changes in training that might prove beneficial to your running and racing performance. And don't underestimate casual advice. People who run with you get to know you—as a person and as an athlete. They can often give you constructive criticism and be great motivators.

I've had several influential coaches in my career. At this point, when I need coaching, my top priority is working with an adviser who is a good sounding board, someone I can bounce ideas off of. Whether it's a coach or personal trainer, find someone whose personality meshes with yours and who you can respect. To find the right person, ask friends, running clubs, health clubs or sign up for a running class. You'll know right away if the relationship clicks. If it doesn't, find someone else.

Finding the Time

Who's not busy these days? One of the biggest challenges for any runner is merely to find time to train. Many of my favorite workouts evolved from my more resourceful attempts to fit them into my day.

Running toward my destination is not only a great time-saver, but it can be a unique challenge. You can do it on the way to anywhere, but one of my favorites is running to the airport. I travel a lot and find I often have to catch an early flight. But I don't like to fly without getting my run in. So I take off for my morning run in the direction of the airport. Scott gives me a 30- to 45-minute lead before he sets out. I tell him my intended route, and he drives until he meets me.

Meanwhile, I attempt to get as far as I can before he arrives. I get a real lift when Scott tells me he's been driving so long and far that he was planning to turn around to see if he missed me! Afterward, I just towel off, often with a wet washcloth I carry in a plastic bag. If I'm still sweating, I put on a dry T-shirt. Then I change my clothes when I get to the airport restroom.

Another practice I've developed is to keep a pair of running shoes, some clothes and a bottle of water in the car. This way, if an opportunity unexpectedly presents itself (like when my car broke down), I can fit in a run. Sometimes I just happen to drive past a beautiful and inspiring area to run. It's nice to know that I'm equipped to go at these times.

One of my most enjoyable workouts was discovered accidentally. I was scheduled to run on the track but my babysitter canceled. So I packed up the kids with toys and bathing suits. It was summer, and the sprinklers at the track facility were on. Abby and Anders spent most of the time playing in the sand in the long-jump pit while Mom did her laps.

In my neighborhood, another option for moms involves using a playgroup as a running group. Two to three women go out for the first shift, while a few remain behind. Then they trade places. It's like a running/babysitting cooperative.

If you're trying to fit your running around your job, then follow the example of the New York Road Runners Club. The club, which is the largest running club in the world, launched a campaign called Run to Work during the New York City transit strike in the 1970s. This popularized a national habit—wearing running shoes to work. You can use a small backpack or leave clothes at the work site. Lobby for a shower facility at your workplace. In the meantime, use a restroom to towel off and change. Or, rent a locker at a nearby health club. Some clubs do not require full membership just for locker-room privileges. You can also run during your lunch hour. Recruit a co-worker or two to join you. Or, reverse the run to work and run home—thus avoiding the "find a shower" problem altogether.

Running in Any Weather

Maine has some of the coldest winters in the country, and some of the warmest and most humid days in the summer. Having trained for marathons in both seasons, I've run the gamut on weather conditions for training outdoors. And I believe that with acclimatization and proper clothing, you can successfully accommodate your running in any climate.

These hot-weather tips are based on expert advice and my personal experience.

• Run in the morning when it's cooler and hopefully less humid. Late afternoon or evening temperatures are better than midday, but summer pollution levels are higher in the evening.

• Stay hydrated. Drink before, during and after your run. Don't wait until you feel thirsty. Also, watery foods such as fruit restore hydration and replace minerals lost through sweat. For drinking mid-run, especially beyond ten miles, you can stash water bottles along the route before you set out or run a course that includes a park or gas station with a water fountain.

• Dress light—in color and material. I wear a light-colored hat to train and race. While you may feel most comfortable in a singlet and shorts, I actually train in a T-shirt—for two reasons. One is that I'm sensitive to the sun, and I need the added protection. The other is that I save singlets for racing; they're part of my "sparest gear," and, if I trained in them, they wouldn't feel as much a part of my racing mode. People may think this is odd, but it has always worked for me, and I don't change what works.

• Protect your skin and eyes. Weather damage is an occupational hazard for any of us out on the roads, especially in the summer. The newer sports sunscreens are designed not to run into your eyes when you sweat. Also, wraparound sports sunglasses may help avoid eye problems from sun exposure.

• Take time to get acclimated. Give yourself one to two weeks to adjust to the heat, whether training or racing. It may happen naturally as the weather warms but be more conservative if you are new to the heat or if there's a sudden hot spell.

• Expect less from your effort. Heat and humidity can be dangerous. Watch for dizziness or feeling extremely hot or even cold—signs of sunstroke. In this case, stop and get out of the sun. While I don't let weather intimidate me, I respect what it can do to the body.

Running in cold weather entails another set of problems. I think one of the worst aspects of winter running is the mental barrier. So my first winter caveat is: Don't look at the thermometer. Reading that number may just sap your determination and cause you to hang up your gear. Besides, the thermometer is not always the most accurate gauge of what it really feels like outside. It doesn't measure windchill, for example.

Part of my winter pre-run ritual is looking for signs—vapor rising on the ocean, frost on certain windows or a furnace that doesn't quit. I enjoy the ritual of judging the weather by these signs. Then I dress accordingly.

Develop your own sense of what's comfortable to wear and rely on several layers that can be removed or put back on, depending on the conditions and your changing body temperature. I often start out wearing an outer sweatshirt or windbreaker that gets stashed along the way; then I pick it up on my way back or later when I'm in the car. (See page 189 for a discussion of winter clothing.)

Watch where you're going. Winter road conditions make it easier to fall or lose control. Particularly with my history of running injuries, I am careful not to run on slippery roads, which cause me to alter my stride. I take the well-worn paths or work out indoors on the treadmill, indoor track, stationary bike or swimming pool.

Tips for Worry-Free Running

Regardless of the conditions, always take the time to remember the basic rules of safe running.

- Run with a partner whenever possible.
- Run facing traffic. Pay attention to passing cars and be ready to literally jump out of the way, if necessary.
- Know the areas where you run. Be aware of any suspicious cars or people who could be tracking you. Leave yourself an escape route, if possible. Avoid isolated dead ends.
- Don't follow the same predictable pattern when you run. I like to vary my routes day-to-day and week-to-week.
- Avoid running alone at night or in the morning darkness.
- Don't count on outrunning a pursuer. In college, I once went out for a late-afternoon run instead of going to a party. A bunch of friends pulled up in a car, chased me down, loaded me into the car and took me to the party. Although my experience was harmless, I realized then that I could always be caught. Endurance means nothing at a time like this.
- Wear reflective gear or bright colors so that you can be seen by passing cars as well as bicyclists. I run on roads with wooded areas

on both sides and need to be seen very clearly, especially during hunting season.

• Let someone know where you're going and how long it should take you. I especially make sure to do this if I am not feeling particularly well. Also, like any outing, it's appropriate to let your babysitter know where you're going so you can be tracked down if necessary.

• In addition to your personal safety, don't forget about home security. If you are leaving the house unoccupied, make sure to lock up.

Running Away from Home

When I'm away from home, I try to find a running partner. I stretch in the lobby of my hotel until someone eventually comes down to run, and I either join them or get advice from the hotel staff on

SAFETY TIPS FOR WOMEN RUNNERS

These running safety tips come from Henley Gibble, Executive Director of the Road Runners Club of America (RRCA), a strong advocate of women's running safety.

• Always stay alert. The more aware you are, the less vulnerable you are.

• Don't wear headsets. Use your ears to be aware of your surroundings.

• Write down or leave word of the direction of your run. Tell friends and family of your favorite running routes.

• Run in familiar areas. In unfamiliar areas, contact a local RRCA chapter or running store. Know where telephones are or open businesses or stores.

• Avoid unpopulated areas, deserted streets and overgrown trails. Especially avoid unlit areas at night. Run clear of parked cars or bushes.

where to run. Sometimes when I'm passing a runner in an unfamiliar area, I'll ask if I can tag along for company.

To be sure I don't get stranded, I stick some money in my shoe or pocket for a phone call or taxi fare, in case I get lost or need a ride. Also, I carry the address and telephone number of the place where I'm staying.

Putting It All Together

As you can see, no matter what your level, training is a holistic process. Lifestyle, training groups, on-and-off mental and physical cycles—not to mention the actual logistics of your running—all blend to create a whole. Your ability to pull them all together will determine your running success. And if you want to translate that success into racing, see chapters 7 and 8.

• Carry identification or write your name, phone number and blood type on the inside sole of your running shoe. Include any medical information.

• Don't wear jewelry.

• Ignore verbal harassment. Use discretion in acknowledging strangers. Look directly at others and be observant but keep your distance and keep moving.

• Use your intuition about a person or an area. React on your intuitions and avoid it if you're unsure.

• Practice memorizing license tags or identifying characteristics of strangers.

• Carry a whistle or other noisemaker.

• Call police immediately if something happens to you or someone else, or you notice anyone out of the ordinary.

Training Charts

Conceived especially for this book, these training charts represent a "meeting of the minds" between Joan Samuelson and John Babington, coach at the Liberty Athletic Club for 19 years. "If I decide to run in the 1996 Olympic trials," says Joan, "John will certainly be one of the first people I'll contact for training advice."

The oldest all-women's running team in this country, Liberty Athletic Club was founded in the 1950s by milkman Bud McManis of Lexington, Massachusetts. Currently numbering between 100 and 150 members, the growth of Liberty Athletic Club has paralleled that of the women's running movement. When the club started, members ranged in age from 8 to 20 but today Liberty Athletic Club is open to all women, and its membership ranges in age from 8 to over 60. The only requirement to join is the desire to train for competition.

Since the mid-1970s, Liberty has attracted the top developing women distance runners in New England including Judi St. Hilaire, Lynn Jennings and Joan Samuelson, all of whom have won several national championships as well as being on several Liberty national championship teams.

Joan represented Liberty Athletic Club until signing with Nike's Athletics West. To this day, she and Babington maintain a close relationship.

A full-time attorney and 2:41 marathoner, Babington has coached the women's track team at Harvard University and currently coaches the Wellesley College women's cross-country team. He has been named assistant coach for the women's track-and-field team for the 1996 Olympic Games, specializing in the 10-K and marathon events. Inspired by Joan's career success, Babington created these training schedules.

Your First 10-K Race

Can you make it through a 10-K? If you're a casual runner doing even 10 miles a week, you can probably survive. But the point isn't to drag yourself through the race. With proper training, you can make it a more challenging experience. This training program—which takes you from 10 to 20 miles per week—is fairly conservative and allows a significant amount of rest (you run only four days a week). The objective of this program is to enable you to cover the 10-K distance comfortably with some strength and speed still in reserve. That way, you can invest a little ambition into your effort.

The Meaning of Strides

Have you ever watched serious runners at a track when they are warming up? After jogging for a while, you'll notice they accelerate on the straightaways. That's striding. It's relaxed, fast running. In other words, you move as quickly as you can without strain while concentrating on good form.

For the novice program, the Tuesday workouts are to be done as strides, which are done faster than your usual training pace. Like a sprint, a stride educates your legs to go faster than your jogging pace. These efforts, however, are not done like repetitions and intervals; you shouldn't time yourself nor should you feel spent after doing them.

If you're not running on a track, pick a running stretch that's flat with no traffic (bikes or cars) to distract you. A smooth surface is important to guarantee good footing. Warm up sufficiently before striding. After each stride, walk or jog a recovery distance equal to that of the stride. As a cool-down, jog slowly for a distance that brings your weekly mileage to the total shown in the chart.

10-K Training Program: Novice Level
See page 79

If you're already running at least ten miles a week or want to work up to that—or if you're fit from another sport—here's Joan's program for a 10-K.

Shown on the chart:

1. Weekly mileage.

2. Tuesday workouts: strides range from 100 meters to 400 meters. Repeat as noted for each week.

Note: Recovery days are very important if you feel you need them.

10-K Program: Race Simulation

In fashioning the 10-K programs for advanced and intermediate runners, Babington drew from the system used by top American 10,000-meter runner Lynn Jennings. A key aspect of these programs is l0-K race simulation. A runner builds up and, at the height of the program, does intervals totaling four to five miles of fast running, broken up into interval segments that alternate short repetitions (400 meters) for pace with longer repetitions (one mile) for sustained effort and rhythm.

This l0-K program is a good combination of tempo running, intervals and races. Babington stresses that the hard session be a quality one. To that end, the schedule allows for significant recovery time.

Doing the main interval workout on the track helps a runner get used to doing laps. This is important for track runners such as Lynn Jennings, who must maintain total focus for 25 laps in a 10,000-meter race.

Why the Blanks?

Only you know how you feel. That's why these innovative training charts allow you to fill in the blanks. Each week features a set of required workouts and a weekly mileage total. After doing the required workouts, complete the week's total mileage according to how you feel, day by day, week by week. Whether it's a rest day or an easy five miles, you'll still get the job done.

10-K Training Program: Intermediate Level
(10-K time between 40:00 and 45:00)
See page 80

Shown on the chart:

1. Weekly mileage.

2. Fartlek sessions: During a distance run, do several speed pickups of varying distances at a brisk pace; jog and return to a normal training pace between speed pickups. It is helpful to pick out a visual target or goal for each interval such as a particular telephone pole.

3. Special 10-K simulation sessions at the track: This workout alternates sets of 400 meters and 1200 meters. It is meant to be fairly challenging. Run 400 meters between your 5-K and 10-K race pace with a short recovery (90 seconds) and do a 400-meter jog recovery after the complete set. Run 1200 meters at the goal 10-K race pace with a 400-meter jog recovery afterward.

4. Tempo sessions: 2½ to 4 miles total, as a continuous run or divided into long segments with short recoveries. At brisk pace or fast cruising.

5. Other interval sessions: Do repeats at your 5-K race pace; recovery interval is approximately equal in time to a repeat run.

Optional: 3 to 10 × 100-meter strides, up to, but no more than, three times a week on easy days after your regular training run.

10-K Training Program: Advanced Level
(10-K time below 40:00)
See page 82
Shown on the chart:

1. Weekly mileage.

2. Fartlek sessions: During a distance run, do several speed pickups of varying distances at a brisk pace; jog and return to a normal training pace between speed pickups. It is helpful to pick out a visual target or goal for each interval such as a particular telephone pole.

3. Special 10-K simulation sessions at the track: This workout alternates sets of 400 meters and miles. It is meant to be fairly challenging. Run 400 meters between your 5-K and 10-K race pace with a short recovery (90 seconds) and do a 400-meter jog recovery after the complete set. Run miles at the goal 10-K race pace with a 400-meter jog recovery afterward.

4. Tempo sessions: 2½ to 4 miles total, as a continuous run or divided up into long segments with short recoveries. At brisk pace or fast cruising.

5. Other interval sessions: Do repeats at your 5-K race pace or faster; recovery is approximately equal in time to a repeat run.

Optional: 3 to 10 × 100-meter strides, up to, but no more than, three times a week on easy days after your regular training run.

Marathon: Consistency Is the Key

When it comes to marathon training, Joan says consistency is the key. That's why this program prescribes the same basic training pattern week in and week out. Using this strategy, do specific workouts on the same days—in these programs, Tuesday, Thursday and Saturday. Joan feels it is important to prepare both body and mind for significant efforts on specific days.

For intermediate and advanced programs, Tuesday is reserved for a speed session, Thursday a medium-long run and Saturday the long run. Joan prefers her longest runs on Saturday for several reasons. She likes to save Sunday as a rest/family day—both spiritually and physically. Second, if bad weather or other conditions prevent a long run on Saturday, the run can be postponed to Sunday without the risk of missing it altogether. Also, Saturday morning may be a good time to run with a training partner who isn't available on weekdays. Consider, too, the back-to-work routine. A Sunday long run can leave you "wasted" on Monday. With the run done on Saturday, a runner can (hopefully) start the week on Monday refreshed.

Since the point of the marathon is to have the strength and confidence to run long, a distinct feature of this marathon program is the two long runs per week with the midweek session slightly less than the main long run on Saturday. To be ready for the marathon effort, Joan is adamant that a runner hit 20 miles at least once in training. "Knowing that you can run 20 miles is a big breakthrough mentally, when it comes to tackling the marathon distance," Joan says.

First, carve out the days reserved for long or hard running; other days, work in distances that enable you to reach the weekly mileage goal. This freedom to go two, four or six miles—poking along, if necessary—eases some of the stress and strain of a set training program. In addition, it gives you a sense of mastery and responsibility in determining a routine based on your own needs. As Joan often stresses, "Only you know how your body feels."

The beginning program focuses on building weekly mileage with two key workouts: a midweek medium-long run and a Saturday long run. There is no hard running and only one 20-miler, about five weeks before the race. The intermediate and advanced programs use the same training patterns, differing only in intensity. If you are planning to compete in races during your marathon buildup phase, replace your midweek run with your long run from Saturday, freeing up the weekend for racing.

Marathon Training Program: Beginner Level
(10-K time 45:00+, experience racing at various distances, preparing for first marathon)
See page 84
Shown on the chart:
1. Weekly mileage.
2. Progression of long runs (see Saturdays).
3. Midweek medium-long run.
Optional: 3 to 10 × 100-meter strides, up to, but no more than, three times a week on easy days after your training run.

Marathon Training Program: Intermediate Level
(10-K time between 40:00 and 45:00)
See page 86
Shown on the chart:
1. Weekly mileage.
2. Progression of long runs (see Saturdays).
3. Midweek medium-long run.
4. Progression of repeat miles: This is meant to be fairly challenging—they should be run faster than your 10-K race pace. Run the fastest average-time possible, while running a consistent time from mile to mile with two to three minutes of recovery.
5. Interval sessions: Distances of 400 to 1200 meters, 2½ to 3 miles total. Babington recommends beginning with longer efforts (1200 meters at approximately a 10-mile race pace) and progress through the workout with increasingly shorter and faster efforts.
Optional: 3 to 10 × 100-meter strides, up to, but not more than, three times a week on easy days after your training run.

Marathon Training Program: Advanced Level
(10-K time below 40:00)
See page 88
Shown on the chart:
1. Weekly mileage.
2. Progression of long runs (see Saturdays).
3. Midweek medium-long run.

4. Progression of repeat miles: This is meant to be fairly challenging—they should be run faster than your 10-K race pace. Run the fastest average-time possible, while running a consistent time from mile to mile with two to three minutes of recovery.

5. Interval sessions: Distances of 400 to 1200 meters, 2½ to 3 miles total. Babington recommends beginning with longer efforts (1200 meters at approximately a 10-mile race pace) and progressing through the workout with increasingly shorter and faster efforts.

Note: As you progress, you may decide to increase your weekly mileage beyond the totals given in the chart. Do what feels right for you. In fact, many elite runners log around 100 miles per week. Keep your longest run at 20 miles, though.

Optional: 3 to 10 × 100-meter strides, up to, but no more than, three times a week on easy days after your training run.

10-K PROGRAM FOR A NOVICE RUNNER

Week	Sunday	Monday	Tuesday	Wednesday	Thursday	Friday	Saturday	Weekly Mileage
1			4		4		4	12
2		3	3		3		5	14
3		3	2 mi. warm-up strides 4 x 100m		4		5	16
4		3	2 mi. warm-up strides 6 x 100m		4		5	16
5		4	2 mi. warm-up strides, 2 x 100m 2 x 200m, 2 x 100m		4		6	18
6		4	2 mi. warm-up strides, 2 x 200m 1 x 400m, 2 x 200m		5		7	20
7		4	2 mi. warm-up strides, 2 x 400m 4 x 200m, 2 x 100m		4		7	20
8		3	2 mi. warm-up strides 4 x 100m		3	2	Rest	12
	Race 10-K							

10-K PROGRAM FOR AN INTERMEDIATE RUNNER

Week	Sunday	Monday	Tuesday	Wednesday	Thursday	Friday	Saturday	Weekly Mileage
1					Tempo			30
2			Fartlek		Fartlek		8	34
3			8 x 400m		Tempo		9	38
4			2 x 400m, 1200m 2 x 400m, 1200m 2 x 400m				9	42
5			Tempo					38
6	Race 8-K				Tempo		10	46
7					2 x 400m, 1200m 3 x 400m, 1200m 3 x 400m		10	42
8			Tempo				9	46

Week				Mileage
9	400m 4 x 800m 400m			42
10	Race 10-K	Tempo	10	46
11		3 x 400m, 1200m 3 x 400m, 1200m 3 x 400m	8	46
12	Tempo			38
13	Race 8-K	Tempo	8	42
14	400m 3 x 1000m 2 x 400m			38
15	Race 5-K	400m 3 x 800m 3 x 400m	7	34
16	400m 3 x 600m 2 x 400m	Race 10-K		24

10-K PROGRAM FOR AN ADVANCED RUNNER

Week	Sunday	Monday	Tuesday	Wednesday	Thursday	Friday	Saturday	Weekly Mileage
1					Tempo			40
2			Fartlek		Fartlek		8	45
3			10 x 400m		Tempo		10	50
4			3 x 400m, Mile 3 x 400m, Mile 2 x 400m				10	55
5			Tempo					50
6	Race 8-K				Tempo		12	60
7					4 x 400m, Mile 4 x 400m, Mile 4 x 400m		12	55
8			Tempo				10	60

Week	Mileage				
9	55			400m / 6 × 800m / 400m	
10	60	12	Tempo		Race 10-K
11	60	10	4 × 400m, Mile / 4 × 400m, Mile / 4 × 400m.		
12	50			Tempo	
13	55	10	Tempo		Race 8-K
14	45			400m / 4 × 1000m / 2 × 400m	
15	40	10	400m / 4 × 800m / 4 × 400m	400m / 4 × 600m / 3 × 400m	Race 5-K
16	30				Race 10-K

MARATHON PROGRAM FOR A BEGINNING RUNNER

Week	Sunday	Monday	Tuesday	Wednesday	Thursday	Friday	Saturday	Weekly Mileage
1							7	25
2				5			8	28
3				6			9	32
4				7			10	36
5				8			12	40
6				8			12	44
7				10				40
8	Race 10-K–20-K			9			14	44

Week								Total
9				10			16	48
10				11			18	48
11				10				44
12	Race 15-K–25-K			10			20	50
13				9			15	44
14				8			10 (unless racing the next day)	40
15	Race (10-K max.)			8			8	34
16	Marathon							20

MARATHON PROGRAM FOR AN INTERMEDIATE RUNNER

Week	Sunday	Monday	Tuesday	Wednesday	Thursday	Friday	Saturday	Weekly Mileage
1							8	30
2			Intervals		7		10	34
3			Intervals		8		12	38
4			3 x Mile		8		13	42
5			Intervals		9		14	44
6			3 x Mile		9		14	46
7			Intervals		10			46
8	Race 15-K–25-K				10		16	50

Week	Race/Event	Workout			Total
9		4 x Mile	11	16	55
10		Intervals	12	18	55
11		5 x Mile	12		50
12	Race 10-K–20-K		10	20	55
13		Intervals	12	18	50
14		3 x Mile	10	14 (unless racing the next day)	42
15	Race (10-K max.)	Intervals	7	10	38
16	Marathon	6 x 400m Easy			30

MARATHON PROGRAM FOR AN ADVANCED RUNNER

Week	Sunday	Monday	Tuesday	Wednesday	Thursday	Friday	Saturday	Weekly Mileage
1							10	40
2			Intervals		8		12	45
3			Intervals		10		14	50
4			3 x Mile		10		15	50
5			Intervals		11		16	55
6			4 x Mile		12		16	60
7			Intervals		12			60
8	Race 15-K–25-K				13		18	70

Week	Race	Workout			Total
9		5 x Mile	13	20	65
10		Intervals	14	20	70
11		6 x Mile	14		60
12	Race 10-K–20-K		14	20	70
13		Intervals	14	18	70
14		4 x Mile	13	16 (unless racing the next day)	60
15	Race (10-K max.)		13	16	55
16	Marathon	8 x 400m Easy			30

CHAPTER 7

JOAN'S TIPS FOR TOP RACING

Pacing for a Strong Finish

*Joan discusses her racing experiences and shares the lessons she has
learned, along with the advice of her coaches, for making the most of
your racing.*

From the very beginning, running to
race was always my goal. I trained in order to compete. For many other
women runners, it's the other way around. First comes running, then
more serious training, and at some point they start to think about racing.

Over the years, I have met a wide range of first-time racers. Some
have been openly elated at the prospect of the racing challenge. Others
have seemed shy and tentative to compete.

Although I'm obviously beyond feeling timid, I can still identify with
those who hesitate. In the early days of my career, I had similar feelings
while running on the roads. I was told that it wasn't ladylike and that a
woman could do herself bodily harm or wouldn't be able to have children. Even today, athletic competition can be a daunting prospect for
some women about to race for the first time.

The excited competitors who attend my clinics sometimes need no advice beyond the encouragement and camaraderie I share with them. And rather than coax apprehensive women out of their shyness, I'm more inclined to simply affirm that their reluctance is part of the experience. After their first race, these women are usually thrilled with the experience and more comfortable with the idea of running future races. Often their reward is all the better by having overcome a significant obstacle.

Racing Readiness

One of the biggest challenges of my career has been timing—specifically, to control and channel my premature adrenaline surges. In the 1984 Olympics, for example, I had to move out of the Olympic Village. Living so closely to the competing and highly successful U.S. swimmers began to unleash my adrenaline a week early!

Once you've trained for a race, you may notice some unexpected physical and emotional results beyond your obvious fitness. From the marathon distance on down, I've experienced similar signs of mental and emotional race readiness. These signs indicate that your engines are revved up and you are excited. Although these feelings can be difficult to endure, they are a positive sign. At the same time, they act as a warning not to go overboard in your training at this point. If they appear prematurely, ease up on your training schedule so you don't peak too soon.

Tapering and Peaking

You have to reach the tip of a mountaintop and then balance there on one foot—that's pretty much what tapering and peaking can be like. Just as you learn to recognize the signs of being "on" in training, you will know when you have achieved a state of optimal race readiness by the feeling that you are "on the edge."

Perhaps the most exciting (and nerve-racking) part of racing happens before you even start to run. That tapering countdown stage between the end of preparation and the starter's gun is a crucial time when your body gears up by fully absorbing your training. Remember, what's done is done. At this stage, any new or extra training cannot help you; it can only hinder your performance.

Tapering gradually brings a racer to the point of peaking. Two of my career highlight races are good examples. I knew I was at peak readiness for both the 1984 Olympic trials and the Olympic Marathon because I didn't sleep well. I was too wound up to get to bed early, and despite a lack of sleep, I eagerly jumped out of bed in the morning, ready to go. During my track workouts leading up to these races I felt superhuman. I would finish a session and be raring to do more. This period of peak fitness is wonderful; you've worked hard to achieve it, and it's an art to peak for just the right moment. But it's also a time to be cautious. For myself, I must be especially careful not to go over the edge in order to avoid injury or burnout. Tapering is the hardest part of marathon training for me.

Peak readiness is not meant to last. You can only be up for a limited amount of time, and it has to be at the right time. When I feel ready to toe the starting line in March and the event is in April, I know I'm at risk. The last time this happened, my resistance dropped and I became sick before the race. In retrospect, this might have happened in the Olympic trials, too, if I had not hurt my knee and been forced to rest. (It just goes to show the cliché is true: Some misfortunes are blessings in disguise.)

Turning ultimate race readiness into success can be so satisfying. But remember, although you may have a particular goal in mind, there are many other victories. You may not run your personal best, but you may finish ahead of people whom you never expected to beat. Or you may finish strongly instead of staggering in.

In my case, some of my best races were those I didn't win. In the 1983 indoor Olympic Invitational 3000 meters, I ran nip and tuck with PattiSue Plumer (several time U.S. champion in the 3000 and 5000 meters) the entire way. I lost by 1/100th of a second but ran what was then my fastest time. I felt the ultimate "runner's high" during this race and was totally satisfied that I got the very most out of myself from the effort.

Strategy and Pacing

Know thyself: That's the best way to plan your race strategy. Have you been speed training? Or racing frequently? Then you can maintain a quicker race pace. Is endurance your strong point? Then be more conservative and hope to pick up the pace and pass people later.

Regardless of the racing distance or your experience, following these basic racing strategies will get you off on the right foot.

Get off the line. Be prepared for a sprint at the starter's gun so as not to get pushed, tripped or boxed in because of the crowd. And know when to fall into your planned race pace. If you're not up to a sprint, stand well back and wait for the crowd to thin out after the start.

Plan your pace. It's easy to get caught up in the excitement of the start. If you tend to go out too quickly, use a strategy to help you control your pace. I might tell a runner in this situation not to reach the two-mile mark before a certain time.

Always plan your race pace based on how you assess your ability and training. A general rule of thumb to judge what your pace should be for, say, a 10-K is to race slightly faster than your usual training pace or a little slower than your speed-training pace. If you train at an 8-minute-a-mile pace, for example, you may be ready to race at a 7:30 pace. Or, if you cover a mile in 7 minutes during your speed workouts, you can expect to race at a 7:40 pace.

Find a friend (or foe). Is there a familiar face nearby? If you race regularly, you'll recognize those competitors who run at a similar pace (a training partner will do). Focus in on them and use them for both pacing and strategic advantage.

Go with the flow. If your adrenaline takes over, and you cover the early miles more quickly than you expected, cut back and concentrate on maintaining your race-pace goal. But more important, don't be afraid to experiment. It's the only way you'll learn and sometimes the only way you can exceed your own expectations. My trademark is to go out at a quick pace, and while I'm by no means recommending it, I believe that my optimism in these situations has allowed me to run fast times and to win races.

Hold your pace. On the other hand, scientific evidence does show that the best results come from running an even pace. Even an attempt at a negative split (a second-half time that is faster than the first) can be a good idea, as is running an even pace. Most personal records are run at an even pace or with negative splits.

Have a plan and stick to it. My strategy has always been to run my own race. That doesn't mean I ignore everyone around me. I always feel things out. I focus on other runners in a pack for a short period of time until I sense that the pace has been established and I feel comfortable and in total control of myself.

Then I tune in to my own strategy and, hopefully, take off. Remember, while others can be a motivating factor, you can't do a single thing about someone else's fitness level, racing style or determination. You can only control yourself.

Use common sense. If you're a novice, combine this advice with some common sense. Don't use a strategy that doesn't feel right for you. Most of all, relax and test the waters. You are going to have to experience various race situations to achieve your personal best.

Set goals for every race. Only you can determine your best personal challenge. Don't let your competition determine that challenge. You have done your homework and only you know what you're capable of. Be realistic but never limit yourself. Just because you find yourself running ahead of someone you've never beat, don't let it throw you. Ride with it.

In the 1983 Boston Marathon, for example, I never expected to run a record pace. It didn't seem possible that I could break a 5:30 pace and run faster than 2:24. Yet I averaged a 5:27 pace and set a course record of 2:22:43, which stood for 11 years. I was never able to duplicate that effort in training.

Recovery: When Rest Is Best

Many times, particularly as a beginner, your race results will clearly reflect your training efforts. The better you train, the faster you race. At some point, however, even though your training is still high quality, perhaps improving, your racing isn't. You don't make a breakthrough. Your running has reached a plateau. But you shouldn't succumb to frustration. Try taking a low-key approach, some R & R. You may surprise yourself—improvement may be just around the bend (so to speak).

In the summer of 1992, I hit just such a plateau, then rallied. As usual for this time of year, my training was flat. Still, I didn't push myself, although that is often hard not to do. I decided to run a low-key five-mile race. My time was equivalent to a low-32-minute 10-K, close to my personal best. The point is that everything will find its own order if, during or after a rough patch, you allow yourself time not just for physical recovery but for mental recovery.

So many runners seem to forget the second half of the training equation: rest. Finding a balance can be most dramatic and frustrating with marathon training. That's why, particularly as a beginner, you should allow yourself plenty of recovery periods between hard efforts, like two or three days between long runs or speed workouts.

When and If to DNF (Do Not Finish)

Midway through a marathon, a sinking feeling takes hold. You're not going to make it—at least not in any meaningful sense. What to do?

As every experienced runner can testify, racing has its trying times. To begin with, you must learn to differentiate between dangerous pain and the natural discomfort from your effort. With training, this comes naturally. Think back to a successful training session like an interval workout. To me, this is the type of pain that "hurts good." It's positive pain. But if this type of discomfort is sapping you during a race, you may need to adjust your pace and bring your efforts more within your comfort zone.

In the meantime, to keep going, find something else to focus on, whether it's the writing on the back of someone's T-shirt, the person you are running next to or the crowd. In my case, people will often yell "Go, Joanie" or even say something totally absurd. I try to take it all in. Tuning into the surroundings, including the crowd encouragement, can be a real pick-me-up. When I am racing well, however, I am totally focused beyond all distractions.

My strongest race asset is my ability to focus mentally. While that focus can be broken, I know how to work to get it back on track again. A race really brings you into the moment. You have to have immense powers of concentration. But, if it gets to the point where physical distress distracts you from your race effort for an extended time and the physical symptoms are worrisome and do not abate, it's probably a good idea to stop.

In the face of no absolute answer, I think you have to judge what feels right. I personally don't stop just because I'm not running well (although there are runners who do and feel it is okay, if necessary), or even if I have discomforting physical symptoms such as cramps. Although I have never DNFed, I think I would know when to stop. I feel strongly that if you feel out of control, if personal health or safety is an issue, then it's time to stop.

What do you do if you can't decide whether or not you should drop out of a race? In long-distance events and at well-organized runs, a medical team will be on hand. You can stop to ask or they will often recognize a runner in distress and intervene. Except for marathons, however, the medical staff is usually present only at the start or finish.

Race Logistics

Getting ready to race is like fine-tuning a car—making sure all the parts are ready to help the engine run smoothly. As the event approaches, it's important to be comfortable with your level of fitness and final preparations. The final week is important, especially before a marathon. You have to generate and store enough energy to be released at the starter's gun. Although I'm notorious for not tapering much before an event, I take my races seriously enough to know when I'm jeopardizing my results and affecting my ability to run well.

I live in an environment that I cherish and in which I am totally comfortable. So I don't like to change my normal daily routine leading up to a race until absolutely necessary.

First of all, I try not to leave home until I have to. If a race is less than a couple of hours from my house, I leave that morning. If it's a couple of time zones away, I try to arrive one day ahead of time. If the race is in another country or more than three time zones away, I like to arrive a couple of days ahead of time to give myself time to adjust.

On the other hand, any race is also an opportunity for a total experience: to travel, see the sights and experience another place or even another culture. In this case, you may want to arrive well ahead of time or plan to stay afterward, regardless of the distance.

Most of the races I run are in the morning. I like to be up and about at least two hours before the start. Although I don't usually take a shower until after my morning training run, I like to shower before a race. It helps me wake up and gives me a feeling of being clean, fresh and ready to go.

Unless the race is after 10:00 A.M., I don't eat anything before the race. I do sip water right up until the start, however, which means that I have to urinate frequently. If the start is late enough to allow food to digest, I have something small and easily digestible, like dry toast or toast with jam and weak tea.

If the race doesn't start right outside my hotel or house where I'm staying, I want to know at least by the night before exactly how I'm going to get there. Being prepared certainly helps make sleeping in a different bed a bit easier. If the race is a mile or so from where I'm staying, I usually jog to the start. But I will gladly accept a ride. Unlike most competitive runners, I don't like to do a lot of running before the race. Nor do I overdo my warm-up. Meanwhile, it seems most of my competition has been warming up forever. Something inside tells me to save it for the race.

On the other hand, you do need to be warmed up before a strong effort like racing. Being warmed up means you break into a sweat. It takes the average person about 12 minutes of exercise to start sweating.

Most of the stretching I do—which isn't all that much unless I'm feeling especially tight or I've noticed other signs of impending injury—is done in the morning after my short warm-up. Again, I don't like to expend too much energy until the starter's gun sounds. Just like I run my own race, I have my own ritual beforehand.

As a last-minute check, make sure your race number is well-pinned and that your clothes are tucked in and your shoelaces are tight. Break in your shoes and clothes ahead of time to make sure nothing chafes. New clothes should be washed a couple of times before a race to soften the fabric.

Some experts recommend that you try to preview a race course ahead of time—especially for a marathon—to know what you'll be facing. While actually seeing a course can be an advantage, it is often impractical. What's more, you can also be well-briefed by studying the race-entry form or map or asking a race official or runner who's covered the course.

While I do take note of where such things as hills and turns are, I personally don't like to see the course. What I don't know won't hurt me. Looking at race courses, especially marathon courses, makes the distance seem so long. "I must be crazy to run so far!" I think to myself. Besides, what's out there that I haven't faced in training? Whatever it is, I'll confront it when I get to it—in my race mode.

CHAPTER 8

RACING DISTANCES

From the Mile to the Marathon

Joan has competed at every racing distance, and here she offers her insight on the advantages of each and the lessons they hold, with some memorable experiences along the way.

Thinking of running a mile or a marathon? Whether your race lasts five minutes or three hours will dictate your racing strategy. Going the distance in the marathon means a very different kind of strength than running the mile. After all, no one worries about whether or not they will finish a mile.

I started out aspiring to compete at the mile and worked up, over various distances, to 26.2 miles. Each distance in between teaches its own lessons, and I've found them all to be valuable every step of the way.

The Mile: A Measure of Any Runner

As the marathon is the classic long-distance event, the mile is a classic track race and the first event that marked my commitment to the sport of running. I started competing in the mile in 1974 as a high-school junior. Only one year earlier, the Maine State Principals Association first allowed girls to run such a long distance. (Now girls this age run the 3000 meters, but in the mid-1970s it was still believed the longer distances could be harmful). That year, 1973, I watched Brook Merrow, now a close friend, win the mile at the Maine State Invitational Meet. Brook's performance so impressed and inspired me that I vowed to become a "real distance runner." "I have to do that," I told myself about running the "marathon" of track and field.

As a miler, I put everything into competing. I won my first state mile championship as a high-school senior, and in the summer of 1975 at the Junior Olympic Nationals, I ran a personal best of 5:01. The following winter I dropped under 5 minutes in an indoor meet. My career best for the distance is 4:36, which I ran in 1983.

A mile is both a challenge and an excellent test of fitness. For a road runner, it is a good way to develop sharpness. As a workout, you can run a measured mile anywhere on the roads. If you want to run an honest mile for time, however, it's best to do it on a track.

If you want to compete at this distance, your training should emphasize speed work with repetitions (interval training). When I was a miler, for example, I did two track workouts a week, with most of the repetitions a half-mile or less. My weekly long run was 10 to 13 miles, while it's nearly double that for a marathon.

For women who run a lot of 5-K (3.1 miles) and 10-K (6.2 miles) races, a mile race is a good test of sharpness. I recommend this, however, only if you've run a mile—or something close to it—in speed workouts, because the mile is a lot shorter and faster than what you're used to.

Running a fast mile before a 5-K or 10-K road race not only can provide the sharpness but can help psych you up, which in turn often motivates you to run a personal record in the longer distances. Dropping down in distance to run on the track during the height of my road racing career in the early to mid-1980s almost always resulted in improvements in my times for longer races.

While you may be scaling down your distance to run a mile, my career evolved by moving up. I ran the mile competitively until after high school. When I first attended Bowdoin College in Brunswick, Maine, which didn't have a women's track program at the time, I kept up my training by running three miles before or after field hockey practice. I would also run with the men's track team during their season and even competed in a few selected men's track meets.

Eventually, I started to challenge myself by running longer distances. I went from 3 miles to 6 and then, not wanting to do the same loop all the time, went to 9. Little could I have guessed at the time, nor could others who knew me, that my ultimate future success would unfold over 26.2 miles. You never know where you'll find your niche. That's why I recommend experimenting with all distances, including the mile.

5 Kilometers: A Great Start

An excellent introduction to road racing, the 5-K is the most popular distance for novices. Women account for 45 percent of the 5-K field, the highest woman-to-man ratio of all the most commonly run road race distances, according to the USA Track & Field Road Running Information Center in Santa Barbara, California. The 5-K is also a good race to sharpen speed if you want to run a fast 10-K.

My best time for the distance is 15:43, which I ran in the 1982 Bislett Games in Oslo, Norway. To illustrate how important experience is, I recall that in this race I went out much too fast. It was my first time on the European track circuit and all the big names in middle distance running were in the race. Before the event, I got overexcited. I'm sure if I had run a smarter race—10 to 15 seconds slower in the early stages—I could have put my fitness to better use and run a better time. This is why it's always good to do a number of races at a given distance to develop your sense of pacing and strategy.

I have found the 5-K to be a good distance to run when I'm gearing up after a rest or a flat training period. For one thing, you can see where you are in your training. It also offers a chance to test and develop leg speed, and the atmosphere of a road race can be an easier introduction to seasonal or beginning speed work than heading to the track. I also like the 5-K because it's one of the few races in which track and road runners meet on common ground with any frequency.

10 Kilometers: A Universal Standard

The 10-K is a popular event on the road race calendar—long enough to get into a rhythm and short enough not to require extraordinary endurance. Many runners find their greatest success at this distance. In addition, I think racing well at the 10-K distance develops the speed and endurance that helps foster success at any distance between 5-K and the marathon.

For me, however, the 10-K can be tricky. In a marathon, you can have a couple of bad miles and still recover. If you fall off the pace, you can pick up time later or legitimately hope to catch up with your competition. If you drop back in a 10-K, it can be very difficult to make up the lost time. For the less competitive runner, a more likely problem would be to go out too fast, then run out of energy during the latter stages of the race.

I can often tell when I'm apt to run a good major 10-K if I have the opportunity to run in a local 10-K (like the Grey Osprey Run or the L.L. Bean Fourth of July 10-K) a week or two before the big race. I'm relaxed and familiar enough with the local runners to know who I should be able to keep up with if I'm in good shape.

If you live in a temperate region, it's fun to take a break from winter and test yourself by traveling to a warm-weather 10-K race. For me, it's an opportunity to get out of the cold, wear some sparer clothing and loosen up my legs. This alone can be inspiration enough to run well, as long as the change isn't too extreme.

7 Miles to 15 Kilometers: Undiscovered Territory

While it can be satisfying to seek perfection at a given distance, such as 10-K, I also enjoy the less commonly run distances between 7 miles and 15-K (9.3 miles). These distances offer variety and ease the pressure of racing for that magic result.

Besides, it's never a good idea to run the same distance all the time. Mixing up the distances serves both to give you a range of conditioning and a better chance to run personal best times. Both the variety and the lack of time pressure are a welcome relief in my running schedule.

By understanding all the factors that may contribute to your racing success, you give yourself the best chance to duplicate that success in the future. For example, when I compare my performances in the Women's Mini-Marathon 10-K in New York City (now the Advil Mini), the Bix 7-Mile in Davenport, Iowa, or the Falmouth Road Race in Massachusetts, I learn something about my strengths and weaknesses. The Advil race is intense—it leaves me feeling drained and overwhelmed. In contrast, I have done very well in the other two races, winning Bix four times and Falmouth six times (more than any other woman). Both are highly competitive events, yet low-key in scope. One is near home and the other is held in a quiet town, with the starting line just a short walk from my hotel room. Nevertheless, thousands of women thrive on the atmosphere of Advil, and Grete Waitz has won the event six times. It just goes to show that it's very individual.

The Half Marathon: A Taste of the Marathon Challenge

Whether you're an experienced marathoner or about to run your first marathon, the half marathon (13.1 miles) offers the best test of your abilities. For an aspiring marathoner, it offers a test in a long-distance run. For the veteran, it's a long-distance race without the commitment to a full 26.2 miles. In fact, the half marathon is good for runners on every point of the distance spectrum. For the 10-K specialist, for example, it's an opportunity to combine speed and strength training over a distance twice as long.

I approach the half marathon as a short-distance race and challenge myself by running it at a pace closer to the 10-K. I try to hold on as long as I can, and when I feel the pace slowing, I tell myself it's not long to the finish compared to a marathon. Then I can usually "smell the barn." I think this confident approach to racing (as opposed to concentrating on surviving) is good for the serious runner. But it's always wise to tie in your approach to your goals and your level of training. That's why for this distance, a cautious approach in the early going is best for all but the experienced runner. If you feel good later, you have plenty of distance in which to pick up the pace.

I have had a great deal of success in the half marathon, particularly the Philadelphia Distance Classic, in which I set a world record of 1:08:34 in 1983. It foreshadowed the marathon success I would have a half-year later in Los Angeles.

One particular half marathon is one of my most personally memorable races. Six months after my son, Anders, was born, Grete and Jack Waitz invited me to run a half marathon in Norway. Initially, I declined, feeling that with a new baby it was too much, but Jack called back to suggest that any boy named Anders should be christened in Scandinavia and that was all it took. At 10:00 A.M. on race day we had a lovely ceremony, and by 2:00 P.M. I had won a half marathon in 1:12:39.

Usually, I get antsy before a race like this, particularly if the field is competitive and I am an invited athlete. I want to make every effort to look good in order to be worthy of the invitation. Sometimes you can spend more energy on worry and nerves than on actual running. In this case, I was more relaxed because I didn't have high expectations for my performance so soon after childbirth. And since there was only an hour between the ceremony and the race start, I had little time to get uptight. Sometimes a distraction is nice. If you face one, don't fight it, go with it. This has taken many years of competitive racing for me to learn.

This Norwegian trip, by the way, was truly a fairy tale holiday—complete with horse-drawn carriage rides, musicians and lavish honors bestowed upon me by the townspeople. In addition, my victory in this scenic race, run up and down the stunning Songa fjords, proved I had fully come back after my second childbirth.

Many runners find combining a race with a trip to be an unforgettable experience. So many new elements come into play. In fact, it can be so inspiring that a group of running friends in New York City, calling themselves the 72nd Street Marathoning and Pasta Club, got together to run marathons around the world. They're so hooked, they're still at it after 15 years.

The Marathon: The Ultimate Challenge

At one point or another, most serious runners want to do a marathon. For many, it is the ultimate challenge. Among first-timers, the majority of people I meet have planned their training carefully and have had some experience running shorter distance races. Occasionally, however, a runner suddenly decides to run a marathon just for the experience. Unless they happen to also be properly trained, I feel these people are not getting all they can out of a marathon.

Like so many complicated endeavors, a marathon is usually not all positive or negative. You may have an overall positive experience running a marathon with negative patches interwoven along the way. You can be tested at any point, not just at the proverbial 20-mile wall. You may end up feeling exhilarated, and yet you will realize your limitations.

Keep in mind that the marathon requires humility and an open mind. I recall one elite runner who, after a string of successes, went into the Boston Marathon convinced he was ready to excel. It didn't work out. He quit the race and didn't run a step for weeks, and I haven't seen his name in any major race results since. I guess he was demoralized and totally unprepared for this down cycle in performance. The marathon can be unpredictable, and some days just aren't your days. But despite the risks, you have to be willing to invest 100 percent of your energy into the event.

I felt that sense of being "off" in the 1989 Boston Marathon. Nothing clicked. I never found a rhythm, never felt fluid or smooth. I was looking expectantly for every mile marker, and my times, as I struggled to reach these landmarks, were disappointing. I ran a terrible race. I just wanted to finish and I didn't care how fast I ran.

Shortly afterward, I became pregnant with my second child, as planned, and in retrospect, I think the fact that my life and my energy were about to be placed elsewhere distracted me from my marathon effort. My training leading up to the event had been a struggle because I was preoccupied. (Yes, some things are more important than running—or at least equally important—even for a serious competitor. While running is my passion, my number-one priority is my children.)

I think a large part of my running success comes from the fact that I've gone with the flow. This is particularly true of the marathon. With this philosophy, you can maintain flexibility. You come to understand that what worked once may not necessarily work at another time. Then, in this zen spirit, you have to accept that there are a myriad of

things out of your control. So many factors affect your race performance—weather, stress, biorhythms and your menstrual cycle. You
prepare as best you can, and then you wake up on race morning subject to some degree of fate. Despite the sense of control that proper
preparation provides, you have to accept that, particularly in the
marathon, the unknown plays a great role.

Are You Ready for a Marathon?

You may have done the work but still aren't sure which marathon
you should run (or if you should run one at all). While I personally
don't favor starting with a big-name race (the logistics are often too
complicated and the media attention makes it hard not to feel pressure), some people are thrilled by big extravaganzas like the New York
City Marathon. You can best assess this by talking to other runners
and reading about or viewing the race you're considering.

How do you train yourself to run 26.2 miles? Such a serious challenge requires very specific preparation.

I think a sensible marathon training program includes a buildup
over six months to a year, with an average of 50 miles per week during
the last two to three months. Some coaches and competitors say you
can do it on less mileage. But I stand by the 50-miles-per-week minimum (60 to 70 miles would be ideal). Contrary to what others may
say, I don't think it's necessary to run more than 20 miles in training. I
think once you have conquered the physical and mental barrier of
running 20 miles, the next 6 miles is nothing (relatively speaking, that
is). Again, too much mileage and you could expend your race effort in
training.

While gearing up for a marathon, I look forward to seeing
improvements from week to week, particularly in my weekly speed
workout. It's important to my mental outlook to see this steady
progress right up until the week of the race, when I might do a workout
of just a couple of shorter intervals (400s, 600s and 800s) to stay physically and mentally sharp. Another gauge of improvement is that longer
runs seem to become easier.

Beware of overtraining and reaching your peak too soon before the
race. This can happen when I get too wrapped up in seeing continuous

improvement and challenging myself. That's because training like this can be enticing and addictive. When I feel this happening, I really have to listen to my training partners, who warn me to cut out of a workout before I go over the edge. Once, I didn't listen and a bad track workout set the stage for a spoiled marathon. I kept trying to make up ground from this one effort, despite the fact that I had been ill and clearly had not recovered.

Despite this failing, when I lined up to run the Boston Marathon in 1993, I was sure I could break 2:30. But I had lost my mental edge from those spoiled workouts and when a warm day dawned, I let the unfavorable weather conditions undermine my confidence. I placed sixth in the race in 2:35:43—a real disappointment.

Don't make this common mistake. Marathon training is very tiring. When you don't feel right, back off. It's all too easy to fall victim to the idea that you *must* run a certain number of 20-milers. When you're tired, it's better to run less.

Don't be afraid to switch training days, either. I once encountered a friend and novice marathoner who was bound and determined to get in a 22-miler on a day when the heat and humidity were at record-high levels. Two days later, the temperature broke. That's when his efforts would have been better spent.

Ironically, some of my best marathons have been when I didn't have complete control of my training during the three months preceding the race—exactly the time when I like to follow a very strict schedule. Examples of these marathons are wins in the Columbus and the Auckland Marathon in New Zealand (both of which I ran in 2:32), and the 1984 Olympic trials and Olympic Games. Sometimes injuries, although demoralizing, are useful because they force you to lay off from intensive training.

Also, running an unplanned marathon or one you don't overly focus on for an extended period of time can be surprisingly rewarding—as long as you have the adequate base training. At least that has been the case for me. In 1980, I ran a marathon in New Zealand on a whim and won it. I was already in New Zealand to run a series of track races when the opportunity to run the Auckland Marathon appeared, and I just went for it.

Marathon Mind Set

The marathon will test your mind as well as your legs. No matter how good your conditioning, no doubt about it, you need an extra measure of confidence for the marathon. Leading up to the race, focus on everything positive about your training and your strength and fitness.

Once you're in the race, imagine yourself back on familiar territory, your home training courses. Think of the race as not one distance but several smaller segments. Try running the first 10 miles thinking about

FOR WOMEN ONLY

Every year, in their June issue, *Runner's World* magazine lists hundreds of women-only races in the country. The top races are ranked for everything from atmosphere and scenery to numbers of participants, top competitors and excellence of organization.

Here are some of *Runner's World*'s top picks, listed by the months they have been run in the past. For exact dates and entry information, send a self-addressed, stamped envelope to the contacts listed below.

Race for the Cure. A series of 56 scheduled races—some coed, mostly women only—designed to promote awareness, education and early detection of breast cancer. Contact the Susan G. Komen Breast Cancer Foundation, Suite 370, 5005 LBJ Freeway, Dallas, TX 75244; (214) 450-1777.

Straub's Hawaii Women's 10-K (March). Contact Straub's Women's Run, Straub Clinic and Hospital, 888 South King Street, Honolulu, HI 96813; (808) 522-4395.

Montana Women's Run 5 Mile (May). Contact Ekkie Wedul, 3412 Ben Logan Lane, Billings, MT 59106; (406) 656-6973.

Mother's Day 8-K for Women (May). Run in Washington, D.C. Contact Washington RunHers, P.O. Box 5622, Arlington, VA 22205; (703) 690-2094.

one of those home loops. When that first portion is done, assess your progress: How long did it take? How did it feel? Your running should still feel easy. Then think of the next 6-mile portion. Tell yourself, as I do, that completing 16 miles seems a lot less than 26.2. I polish off that portion and gear up mentally for the last 10 miles, when it's especially important to stay upbeat. I put myself back on one of those familiar home courses, clicking off the miles. "Hey, this isn't so bad," I tell myself, and I continue to keep focused on positive (but realistic) thinking.

Advil Mini-Marathon 10-K (June). Bills itself as the original and most prestigious women-only road race in the country. Contact the New York Road Runners Club, 9 East 89th Street, New York, NY 10128; (212) 860-4455.

Alaska Run for Women 8-K (June). Contact Jeni Winegarner, P.O. Box 112727, Anchorage, AK 99551; (907) 345-5767.

Brueggar's Run for the Bagels 10-K and 5-K (June). Contact Marcia Dunn, 5221 43rd Avenue S, Minneapolis, MN 55417; (612) 724-7505.

Freihoffer's 5-K (June). Run in Albany, New York. Contact George Regan, 233 Fourth Street, Troy, NY 12180; (518) 273-0267.

Lady Foot Locker 5-K (June). Contact Event Sense, Inc., 219 East Seventh Avenue, Denver, CO 80203; (303) 863-1633.

Tufts 10-K (October). Contact Andrea Mrusek, Conventures, Inc., 250 Summer Street, Boston, MA 02210; (617) 439-7700.

Danskin Women's Triathlon Series. A series of swim, bike and run events from July through September in six locations. 1-800-452-9526.

For the Serious Marathoner

I've never met a first-time marathoner who didn't swear "never again" right after the race. After the 1979 Boston Marathon, my first true marathon (I had run one other as a training run in Bermuda after a competitive 10-K), I, too, said the same thing, despite the fact that I won in an American record of 2:35:15.

It only takes one night, usually right after the race, to start thinking about how you might have run better, how you could change your training and where you might do it. I always have trouble sleeping the night after a marathon. Instead of "never again," I'm usually saying to myself, "Next time. . . ." Once the distance has been completed, the challenge shifts to seeing how fast you can cover it.

A serious marathon—one in which you run for time—is often the goal for a woman who has completed the distance, and it's the next logical step for the serious athlete who has competed at shorter distances. For this athlete, I feel that it's necessary to have a base maintenance of 25 to 35 miles per week, reaching 55 to 60 miles per week during the last few months of serious marathon preparation.

Just like all the distances mentioned in this chapter, after you've had the experience and gained the confidence, you're ready to go for it.

Choosing the Race That's Best for You

For women, the running boom is alive and well. According to the USA Track & Field Road Running Information Center, in the early 1990s, more than 1.2 million women ran road races in the United States. As you read this, more are joining their ranks.

As women runners, you face a unique choice, particularly if you are new to racing. Should you choose an all-women's race? Although there are pluses and minuses to any event, as a competitive runner, I prefer mixed-gender races. In all-women's events, I lose a lot of energy focusing on the other women. It's harder for me when there is no place to hide. In a mixed race, you can play hide-and-seek, positioning yourself amidst packs of men to help you set your pace or open up a gap. (On the negative side, of course, a woman can lose track of her competition in the pack.) Because I feel no competition with the men, I can take a break from the intense energy competition requires and from continually calculating: Where am I? How am I doing?

There's a tremendous sense of camaraderie in all-women's races. A lot of women feel inferior or uncomfortable in a race where they're surrounded by men. They may have the opposite problem from me: They are more distracted by the men than the women. Also, the clinics offered at all-women's races allow the women a freedom to communicate that I don't see in mixed clinics, which are focused on the average runner, meaning the average male runner.

I think of races like the Tufts 10-K in which the lead pack passes the rest of the runners as they head back toward the finish. The cheering and support is just incredible. It is so uplifting for runners in both the front and back of the pack to see each other. The same is true of passing Wellesley College on the Boston Marathon course and feeling the rush of the women cheering. Women have a real desire to celebrate other women.

CHAPTER 9

WHEN THINGS GO WRONG

Overcoming Injuries

Injuries—they can perplex you, obsess you and lead you on a seemingly endless search for a cure. Nearly every runner, man or woman, will encounter a running injury at some point. And few people know better than Joan Samuelson what it's like to live with—and overcome—these occupational hazards of running. Yet, you can run without injury if you train properly and follow a few guidelines.

"I've had more than the average number of injuries for an elite runner," claims Joan, a contention that no one would contradict. During the 1980s, Joan had surgery on both Achilles tendons—twice—and arthroscopic surgery on her right knee. When you add in nonrunning-related operations—like an appendectomy and two hernia repairs—it's quite a collection. In fact, Joan literally keeps track of her surgeries by reading her scars like a road map. And keep in mind that surgery is a last resort. Considerable aches and pains preceded her operations.

Why has Joan been so injured—build, biomechanics, bad luck? Probably none of the above. "I think it was because I was pushing myself so hard. I probably ran more mileage, at a harder pace, than most of my competitors. And a leg-length discrepancy from an early skiing accident didn't help."

We hear a lot about great mentors and coaches, but an athlete's medical corps can be just as essential to her career. Joan first met Robert Leach, M.D., through her coach, John Babington, in 1977. A decade later, he performed several of her surgeries. He was then chairman of the Department of Orthopedics at University Hospital in Boston. Currently, he is the editor of the *American Journal of Sports Medicine*.

How does Dr. Leach assess Joan's injury history? For one thing, he believes her skiing accident has contributed to her subsequent running injuries. For the most part, though, what did her in was the intensive training. "I don't think many people truly understand what it means to run 110-mile weeks and to do a lot of those miles fast. Considering how hard she worked, Joan actually did amazingly well."

The Joan Samuelson writing this book is a seasoned athlete who understands sensible training and balancing life and sport. Now, when necessary, she allows herself easy running days. But at her peak, she would frequently run a race during a 110-mile week—which meant no pre-event tapering or rest. Characterized by two daily runs, morning and afternoon, her week would often include a 15-miler, 20-miler, a track workout and a timed 10-K. Before an intense afternoon track workout, she would often run 10 to 12 miles in the morning. And she never ran slowly.

"I ran with a good, strong effort in the morning and put whatever I had left into my afternoon run—pushing myself to give the best possible effort to each session," says Joan. She concludes, "I simply felt good all the time. I would just push to the limit, then get injured and find an alternative to stay in shape until I healed." In retrospect, it's not a strategy she would recommend.

Who Gets Hurt and Why?

So why do some people seem to suffer more injuries than others? "We don't know," says Dr. Leach. "We can only guess. We think that the biomechanics of how people run plays a role, but there is no good evidence to support that. We do know that if you work hard, it increases the odds of breaking down."

In Joan's case, says Dr. Leach, "She just ran incredibly hard and once broken down or injured, because of competition, she did not have the luxury of giving herself time to heal. On the other hand,

MAN OR WOMAN—WHO'S AT RISK?

The old-fashioned notion that women runners are more prone to injury is just that—old-fashioned. And wrong. According to Robert Leach, M.D., editor of the *American Journal of Sports Medicine* and formerly chairman of the department of orthopedics at University Hospital in Boston, "Among the elite there is little basic difference in type or rate of injuries. The truth is, except for bigger muscle mass in men and a wider pelvis in women, the male and female anatomies for running are similar.

"As information on female athletes accumulates, we'll be less likely to label running injuries as gender-specific. The idea that there are more stress fractures in women or more muscle pulls in men, for example, will fade, particularly as girls begin athletic training earlier—starting at age 13 or so."

"What's more," he adds, "we'll have the chance to study some long-term effects of lifetime training. How might early involvement of females in sports and physical activity affect diseases such as osteoporosis in later life, for example?"

"My wife, Laurie, is a case in point," says Dr. Leach. "A U.S.-ranked tennis player, runner, skier and mother of six, she's a 5-foot-7, 129-pound woman in her fifties. A test showed her bone mass to be comparable to that of a 32-year-old woman. It's a good bet that in addition to good genetics, her lifelong physical activity is the reason."

Bill Rodgers, four-time winner of both the Boston and New York City Marathons, was almost phenomenal in his ability to remain un-injured."

Injuries from the Ground Up

Joan has learned about injuries the hard way—through personal experience. Here, she takes you on a tour of common running injuries, accompanied by Dr. Leach's explanations and recommendations for care and prevention.

Toenail troubles. "A long, hard run can leave you with painful or blackened toenails," says Joan. "Nails are damaged by impact when toes are jammed into the front of the shoe while running. A variety of training errors may be to blame: running on the crown of the road, an altered foot plant to avoid another injury or a shoe that's one size too small. Sometimes, especially while running hard, you can get 'beyond the pain' and not realize you have a bad nail (or blister) until you take off your shoes. It initially turns red and can be extremely sensitive. By the time the blood under the nail turns black, the pain is usually gone.

"When it's really painful, I pierce the nail with a sterile needle and let the fluid seep out to relieve the pressure. If it's particularly bad, I cut off the top of the running shoe where the toenail hits. When toe-nail pain keeps recurring, I've known runners who solved the problem by switching to a slightly larger running shoe."

Blisters. "Blisters can come from any irritation," says Dr. Leach, "shoes too loose, too tight, poorly fitting shoes or wet socks, bony spurs on toes. . . ." The list goes on and on. The friction or pressure creates heat and fluid accumulates under the skin.

Nearly every runner has had blisters, and Joan is no exception. "I've gotten blisters from something rubbing against the foot, from the irritation of hot pavement and because of a bony protrusion. You can also get blisters from wet socks—like if you're hosed down during a race.

"As soon as I know I have a blister, I take off the shoe (or shoes). If the blister is large and painful and I can't stand the pressure, I pop it with a sterile needle and get out as much fluid as possible. (Not all doctors advocate this step, however.) Then I apply an antiseptic and cover the blister with an adhesive bandage or gauze and tape. Once it begins to heal, I expose the blister to the air as much as possible so it can dry out and heal completely." Dr. Leach advises leaving the top layer of skin intact after you've let the fluid out or as long as the underlying layer is still tender.

As for preventing blisters in the first place, Joan says, "I try to avoid blisters by moving my toes and not letting a potential 'hot spot' develop. A good preventive measure, which I use especially before a marathon, is to rub petroleum jelly all over my toes and feet. This works particularly well for me." (Don't try this in a marathon if you've never tried it in training—on a long training run, for instance.)

"Another source of my blisters, believe it or not, is dress or casual shoes. As runners, we are usually supercareful about the proper fit of our running shoes, but I, for one, often don't take equal care with choosing other shoes. You can't get away with an ill-fitting dress shoe for very long before it becomes a problem.

"I recently found a comfortable pair of dress shoes and did what I do when I find a good sports shoe—I bought three pairs of them."

One more thing: Remember to smooth out any folds in your socks before putting on your running shoes. Also, check out the wide variety of socks designed to protect runners' feet. Some are marketed as specifically blister-proof. (See page 192 for more on socks.) But nothing is guaranteed blister-proof, says Dr. Leach, who suggests running with two pairs of socks—one very thin. Nevertheless, a good shoe fit is the best insurance against blisters, he adds.

Achilles tendinitis. Your calf muscles are attached to your heel by the Achilles tendon. As you propel yourself forward in running, the muscles tighten and the tendon sheath may become irritated and subsequently inflamed (Achilles tendinitis). In some advanced cases, such as Joan's, the tendon actually degenerates.

When Dr. Leach treated Joan for Achilles tendinitis, she was also very inflexible in this area. Because the tendon is forced to stretch with every running stride, inflexibility contributes greatly to this injury. And even more so with fast running. Were Joan's inflexible Achilles tendons inherent or because of lack of stretching? "I can't be sure," states Dr. Leach, "because by the time I first saw Joan at age 18, her Achilles tendons were already tight."

Joan describes her painful condition: "It was so bad that if Scott accidentally kicked my leg in his sleep, I would go through the sheets. I had to put on shoes just to go to the bathroom in the middle of the night—walking barefoot was just too painful without the lift of shoes.

"I had surgery on both of my Achilles tendons twice—first in 1982 and again in 1985. Surgery helped, especially the removal of degenerative tissue, but the problem returned. I still wonder why. Is it genetic? Structural? My leg-length discrepancy? Inadequate stretching? I'm not sure and neither are my doctors. As with my other injuries, the most logical explanation seems to be overuse.

"As for prevention and solutions, stretching can help as well as icing. Although a bit painful, I have found that friction massage (fast strokes to heat the muscle) is an excellent way to break up the scar tissue. Of course, I would recommend any of these methods before ever considering surgery."

Joan's problem is not unique. Dr. Leach knows of at least ten elite runners who have needed reoperations on their Achilles tendons. But now, more than a decade after Joan's surgery, runners are more enlightened, says Dr. Leach. "The learning curve has improved since those earlier days of Joan and her peers." They recognize when they are in trouble and back off, so fewer runners need this surgery.

Joan notes that she had chronic Achilles problems right up until her first pregnancy. She has had only minor problems or slight sensitivity since pregnancy and breast-feeding. She speculates that the pregnancy hormone relaxin may make a difference. Confirms Dr. Leach, "This hormone causes the basic structural tissue of the tendon to be more elastic. While we know this causes a change in the pelvis, it is unlikely the change applies only to that area. Surely other tissues in the body benefit."

Plantar fasciitis (arch pain). Extending across the bottom, or sole, of the foot, the plantar fascia is a band of tissue that connects the heel and the forefoot. Because this area is always under stress, even when walking but particularly when running, inflammation is fairly common, says Dr. Leach. This is one injury, though, that Joan has escaped.

The pain is often severe in the morning. Then it begins to feel better when starting a run, only to become much worse after three to five miles. Stretching the Achilles tendons helps, and in the case of pain, use ice after running. As a massage, rolling your foot over a golf ball can provide relief. Dr. Leach also suggests wearing shoes with good support, possibly with orthotics, or taping the foot and using a felt-pad insert. In any case, your best bet is to consult a podiatrist.

Other foot problems. When you run, each foot absorbs the impact of up to five or six times your body weight as it hits the ground. So a small problem or tiny defect in your foot can have a big impact on your running.

As an example, Joan had a sesamoid bone under her big toe removed because it caused severe pain in the midfoot area when she landed. It was removed at the same time Dr. Leach performed her second Achilles tendon surgery.

During running, the feet tend to roll inward on impact, or pronate. Runners often believe any pronation is bad, but in fact, some pronation is normal. For women (and men) who do overpronate, however, a good arch support is critical.

Another problematic foot flaw is Morton's toe, a second toe that is longer than the first. This irregularity can affect balance and foot plant while running. Deb Merrill, a certified neuromuscular therapist in private practice in Brunswick, Maine, says that runners with Morton's toe, overpronation or excess supination (rolling onto the outside of the foot) may experience weak ankles that sprain easily, low back pain, arch fatigue, foot pain, shin splints or pain on the outside of the calf (peroneal muscles). If you encounter these problems or other difficulties with your feet, consult a sports medicine specialist or podiatrist.

Occasionally, a runner will develop a neuroma, or painful inflammation and swelling of the nerve between the toes, usually between the third and fourth toes. To ease the pain, Dr. Leach recommends using a pad in the shoe between the metatarsal heads of the toes involved (sometimes it's hard to place the pad accurately). Other possible treatments involve steroids injected into the local area where the nerve is inflamed or surgical removal of the nerve. Either way, medical help is called for.

Shin splints. Runners often refer to any pain in the front of the lower legs as shin splints. This inflammation can be caused by many things—overtraining, intense training after a hiatus or shifting to a harder running surface.

"I have had only a minor encounter with shin splints," says Joan, "but it was a great lesson. When I was in college, I remember constantly hearing runners complain of shin splints. I thought they were a bunch of wimps, until I got them myself. I never hurt so much! During my year at North Carolina State University, I was running on several different surfaces, from cross-country to track to the roads—and radically mixing the efforts from slow to fast and in between. The best way I found to deal with the problem was ice massage."

According to Dr. Leach, the best cure for shin splints is rest (or cross-training). Some support, like taping, can help. So can trying to support the muscles around the tibia by wrapping an elastic bandage around the leg. Sometimes taping the calf muscles by starting in the back and bringing the tape forward brings relief. You usually need a trainer to do this properly.

Stress fractures. Normally, walking or training fosters the normal course of repairing, building and replacing bone. "For some reason—and we don't know exactly why—in a stress fracture, bone breaks down faster than it's rebuilt," says Dr. Leach. More women than men suffer from this problem, perhaps because women have less muscle mass than men to protect the bone, speculates Dr. Leach. Interestingly, while this increase in women seems to be the case for stress fractures, it is not true for shin splints.

"Shin splints do not lead to stress fractures, but the two are often confused," states Dr. Leach. "A bone scan will reveal a stress fracture, which needs about eight weeks of rest to heal." The key to avoiding this problem, he says, is to monitor training closely and pay attention to any bone tenderness—an early warning sign—and back off.

Knee pain. "The knee is probably the most common site of pain in runners," notes Dr. Leach, "but any number of problems may cause knee pain, so making the right diagnosis can be tricky."

Joan's story bears this out. "A knee injury is the ailment for which I am most famous. It happened in 1984, and at the time, it seemed like a real fluke. Suddenly, during one run, I remember it felt like something was unraveling and spiraling down on the outside of my right knee. I had trouble moving and couldn't bend or extend my leg without pain. At the time, I was training for the Olympic trials marathon, and I immediately called Dr. Leach in Boston.

"I swore I'd never take a shot of hydrocortisone but that's what Dr. Leach recommended. I was closing in on the trials, which I had been aiming for since the women's Olympic Marathon was announced three years earlier. Dr. Leach gave me my first shot of hydrocortisone into the painful area, but it didn't relieve the problem. I had a second shot a week later and that didn't seem to work, either. Then I knew I was in trouble.

"Dr. Leach thought the scar tissue in the knee was inflamed, so he put me on a course of anti-inflammatory medication. That didn't help at all. I wasn't surprised. As a runner, I've become so in tune with my body that I can at least sense the source of things. It didn't feel like an inflammation; it felt like a kink.

"While on a West Coast speaking engagement, I went to Eugene, Oregon, to seek treatment from Rich Phaigh, the massage therapist with Athletics West, an elite running team. After a couple of sessions with Rich, he realized he couldn't help. I was running out of time. He suggested I consult Stan James, M.D., an orthopedic surgeon (also in Eugene). At that point, it was a real race against the clock. Dr. James eventually performed arthroscopic surgery 17 days before the trials."

What Dr. James found in Joan's knee was a fibrous degeneration of the plica, a fold of tissue that normally extends across part of the knee joint from the side wall to the kneecap. "Sometimes it becomes irritated by rubbing across part of the knee joint and degenerates into rough fibrous tissue, causing considerable pain," explains Dr. Leach.

"We don't see a lot of problematic plica in runners. If Joan's problem had merely been inflammation, the hydrocortisone would have worked," says Dr. Leach. "Because the tissue had became more fibrous, however, only surgical removal could help. And Joan's problem was that she could not afford to give it adequate rest. She was coming up on the Olympic trials."

Runner's knee. Joan has had her share of knee problems, including some minor chondromalacia (kneecap damage caused by wear and tear). As Joan reports, "My bout of runner's knee appeared early in my running career and was very short-lived. I just took some time off and it healed."

Technically speaking, runner's knee isn't a medical diagnosis but a commonly used term for a variety of problems—half a dozen or so, according to Dr. Leach. "All the more reason for runners to seek a sports medicine professional who can make a specific diagnosis and prescribe specific treatment." He recommends seeking treatment if knee pain continues for four days to one week and if it worsens. The good news is, according to Dr. Leach and other experts, runner's knee does not lead to arthritis.

Iliotibial band syndrome. The iliotibial band (ITB) runs along the side of the leg from the hip to a point just beneath the knee. Because this band of tissue stabilizes the knee during side movements, problems with pronation or inflexibility can irritate it and cause considerable pain. With ITB syndrome, this band rides over and back across a small bony knot on the outside of the knee during the constant flexion and extension that occurs while running.

Runners with ITB syndrome should cut back on training, stay off hills and use an anti-inflammatory (such as ibuprofen), advises Dr. Leach. Specific stretches to promote flexibility (see chapter 10) and weight training to strengthen the area (see page 148) can help.

Hip pain. With runners, a hip injury is rather uncommon and hard to diagnose precisely, says Dr. Leach.

Wider hips in women are often blamed for specific injury problems elsewhere. He comments, "There is no question that a wider pelvis will cause certain knee problems, such as chondromalacia." Wider hips also increase the angle at which the runner's foot strikes the ground, so pronation can be exaggerated.

Other hip-related problems may come from overuse. Says Dr. Leach, "I have seen an awful lot of women who achieve cardiovascular conditioning very easily, and thus increase their training quickly. Because the tissues, however, have not had sufficient time to adapt to training, breakdown may then result."

Leg muscle strains. Explosive activities and sports, like sprinting, tennis or basketball, lend themselves to muscle strains, says Dr. Leach. "Distance running, where the activity is very rhythmic, is less likely to cause this problem. That's one of running's nice qualities," he adds.

Other muscle problems are simply classic muscle soreness. In any case, be careful to warm up before any hard running, especially when muscles are tight, to avoid the possibility of muscle strains.

Sciatica. Strictly speaking, sciatica is a symptom, not an injury—

a sharp, stabbing pain felt anywhere along the sciatic nerve, which runs from the lower spine down the back of the thigh and onto the foot. Sciatic pain is associated with a wide variety of back conditions, since any number of disruptions or biomechanical faults can irritate the sciatic nerve and create pain.

According to Dr. Leach, possible causes include a ruptured disk, irritation by small spurs in the lower lumbar spine or a deformity in the spine—all of which can be aggravated by running.

When pain is sharp and disabling, rest is the most helpful therapy until the irritation subsides and a diagnosis can be made, says Dr. Leach. Most experts feel back problems initially need a very careful physical exam. Then "corrective exercises are the biggest help." These strengthening exercises for the surrounding muscles help prevent future episodes.

Runner, Heal Thyself

In the beginning, runners had only themselves to turn to when confronted with aches and pains. The doctors offered no more than the traditional advice: If it hurts, stop running. As the field of sports medicine expanded, new therapies emphasized balanced muscular strength and flexibility and the value of ongoing conditioning through stretching, massage and cross-training.

To stay abreast of new healing techniques, Joan relies on neuromuscular therapist Deb Merrill. When counseling runners, Merrill advises that with proper rest and self-care most injuries to soft tissues like muscles, tendons, ligaments or connective tissue (as opposed to bone) will ultimately heal themselves with or without professional care. If the self-care techniques outlined here, however, do not yield results in about two weeks, see a doctor. They may be bone or joint problems.

In day-to-day maintenance, the following things are important to remember.

• Listen to your body. Use your training diary (as discussed on page 55) to monitor changes and discern patterns.

• Pay attention to early-warning tightness and aches or pain.

• Treat injuries as soon as possible.

For new pain or injuries, follow the classic RICE treatment (rest, ice, compression, elevation). According to Michael Sargent, M.D., team physician at the University of Vermont in Burlington, you should apply RICE as follows:

• Rest the injury until the initial inflammation subsides, usually 24 to 72 hours.

• Ice it three times a day for about 20 minutes. Be sure to protect the skin from direct contact with the ice pack.

ICE IS NICE

Ice packs are standard equipment for active exercisers and athletes. But if an ice pack is too messy, too cold or otherwise inconvenient or uncomfortable, you're not as likely to use it. To make your own flexible slush pack for just pennies, try this recipe.

¾ cup water
¼ cup rubbing alcohol
2 resealable sandwich-size plastic bags

Put the water and alcohol into a resealable plastic bag (the better the quality of the bag, the longer it will last without leaking). Push out the bubbles and zip up. Seal within a second bag and freeze.

Use this bag of frozen slush on any sore area. It's best to wrap a damp towel, even a paper towel, around the ice pack when applying it to your skin. Moist cold (and moist heat, too) penetrates deeper than dry cold, and the towel will protect your skin from freezing. Be careful your skin does not turn white. Apply for no more than 15 minutes.

As another useful alternative, freeze paper cups of water to use for ice massages. Peel back the paper cup as you rub the ice on the area. In a pinch, you can use a bag of frozen vegetables as an ice pack.

- Compress it with an elastic bandage or tape.
- Elevate the injured area at a level higher than your heart to keep swelling down.

Take ibuprofen to further reduce inflammation and pain. (Ibuprofen can cause stomach upset in some people.)

Stretching: An Ounce of Prevention

You've been told to stretch by everyone—runners, coaches and doctors. Stretching is a universal prescription as part of a running program—and for good reason. According to Merrill, stretching warm muscles is one of the best ways to prevent injury. That's because an elongated, flexible muscle can fully and easily contract and relax as you run. In contrast, a shortened, inflexible muscle can be strained when pushed beyond its limited range of motion during running.

Sudden painful injuries, of course, should never be stretched. At least half the runners who come to Merrill have done more harm than good, launching into a vigorous program of stretching after injury, retearing the muscle in the injured area. Instead, let the area heal with rest (and possibly massage). Maintaining range of motion without placing stress on the area is helpful but avoid any intensive stretching for a couple of weeks.

After the first 48 hours of a serious injury, Merrill highly recommends massage to increase circulation and reduce muscle spasms in the injured area. (Chapter 10 covers all the benefits of both stretching and massage.)

Self-Care: The Key to Injury-Free Running

Don't let Joan's knee story frighten you. Often, if you're careful, you can take care of any initial sports aches with preventive measures: ice, rest, cross-training, exercises to support the surrounding muscles and avoiding certain surfaces when running.

Merrill offers some additional tips for self-maintenance.

Raise your legs. After running, especially a hard workout, raise your legs against a wall to assist circulation back to the heart. This reduces excess swelling in the legs, which can sometimes damage muscle fibers, and it also flushes out the by-products of exercise such as lactic acid. "Indeed, many coaches refer to this technique as flushing," says Dr. Sargent.

Choose wet over dry. When treating an injury, remember that moist heat and moist cold penetrate better than dry. A hot-water bottle provides dry heat, for example. Instead, try a moist towel wrapped around a cold or hot pack or a wet towel.

Give 'em the cold shoulder. When you feel any new pain or tightness in your muscles, however minor, try applying ice or ice massage for 20 minutes twice a day for two days.

Warm up twice. If muscles are tight or you're recovering from an injury, before exercising, apply moist heat for five to ten minutes to warm the muscle and increase flexibility. This will also lessen the chance of further muscle injury.

Don't premedicate. Too much of a good thing is still too much. Some runners take ibuprofen or aspirin before a race in hopes of preventing post-race soreness or to lessen aches and pain during the run. Both Merrill and Dr. Sargent advise against it. "A drug that masks pain can allow you to do further damage to an injury," Dr. Sargent points out.

Do evaluate. Even if you usually stretch after you exercise, it's a good idea to pause five minutes into your run and briefly stretch your calves, quadriceps and hamstrings. This lets you assess your muscle flexibility for the day.

Be prepared. A thorough warm-up and stretching are especially important for speed work and hills—which require a fuller range of motion. A stretching break may also help during long runs, when muscular fatigue sets in.

Good Form: Special Advice for Women Runners

Women's hips are generally wider than men's and tilted forward from the waist, Merrill contends. "That tilt is what often gives them biomechanical problems as runners. Many women runners have this forward tilt, which may be exaggerated by childbirth, as in Joan's case, but genetics has a strong influence."

Keeping good form while running trains your body to stay in

alignment and thus lessens the chance of injury. Here's how to check your alignment as you run.

Run straight and tall. Because of the forward pelvic tilt, Merrill feels it is especially important for women to concentrate on maintaining an upright stance when they run. Tuck in your butt, lift your knees and hold your head "floating" above your body toward the sky. Your head should feel weightless and light, uplifted with the rest of the body "suspended" underneath.

To see how fatigue causes a forward lean at the waist, and thus an inefficient gait, just watch middle- and end-of-the-pack marathon runners. "Other runners tend to lean backward and pull their arms up when fatigued," points out Dr. Sargent. "Either deviation from 'running tall' wastes energy." (To work on this problem, try the drills in chapter 11.)

Swing your arms. As they run, some women tend to cross their arms alternately in front of their chests, rotating their forearms inward with the back of their hands facing forward. "Often in this position the wrists flex downward in what is called the pocketbook posture," says Dr. Sargent. "This form is biomechanically inefficient and creates a great deal of tightness. Instead, women who run this way need to develop a relaxed, pendulum-type arm swing to balance the leg motion of running."

To work on proper swing, try practicing the following drill from Merrill—called happy thumbs—in front of a mirror: Hold the hands in a loose fist, sticking the thumbs straight up. Bend the elbows at a 90-degree angle and keep the thumbs pointing toward the sky. Swing each hand down alternately, brushing past the upper thigh. Once you've perfected the swing, relax your thumbs but make sure they always face upward.

Check for proper foot plant. When some women run, because their hips are wider than men's and they tend to tilt forward, their feet may land too close to the center of the stride, creating buttocks muscle problems and an imbalance in the inner and outer thighs. "This can be worsened by tight inner thigh muscles—a good reason for doing a groin stretch," says Dr. Sargent.

If your feet are lined up correctly under your hips, they should not cross over the midline of your stride when running. To check this, run in the sand (or anywhere you can make a footprint) and then check to make sure your feet fall on either side of a straight line. Also, check the sides of your running shoes to see if there are any scuff marks—a sign that one foot is actually hitting the other. If your feet are not landing correctly, consciously work on adjusting your stride so your legs are better aligned under your hip sockets. This can help sore knees as well.

A Final Word on Staying Healthy

What's a good guide to injury prevention? Your own training log. It shows how you run, charts any patterns that could lead to injury and, if you do get hurt, details how you recovered. That's why studying your training diary is one way to keep history from repeating itself.

Getting injured—or avoiding injury—depends on a long list of factors. Every runner is different. So knowing how to listen to your body is important in staying healthy. No matter what your physical shape, being "body wise" will help you heal fast—and, even better, avoid injuries in the first place.

CHAPTER 10

STRETCHING

The Key to Running Longevity

Frankly, Joan doesn't like to stretch. But she's learned a lot about what happens when you *don't* stretch.

During her career, Joan's habit was to run until she got injured, stop, recover, then repeat the cycle all over again. Her doctors seem to believe that had Joan stretched regularly, there's a good chance she could have avoided at least some of the injuries that interrupted her training over the years.

Sound familiar? If you forget to stretch or you put it off, you can probably identify with Joan. Although she no longer ignores her need to stretch, her practice still waxes and wanes. Fortunately, she does get massages regularly when training, which help. And she has gotten more careful about her flexibility as she's gotten older, as most of us should. So you might say the theme of this chapter is: Don't learn the hard way.

Why Stretch?

Picture yourself coming home after a long run. You pour yourself a tall glass of water or sports drink, maybe a second, but before you can stretch and get into the shower, the phone rings. About 35 minutes later, you've settled the crisis of the moment—you head upstairs for the shower, but your legs are so tight they feel like they're in plaster casts. What happened?

This is a classic case of exercised muscles getting tighter as they cool down after an effort like running. And the harder your muscles have worked, the tighter they seem to get. Exercise is not the only thing that causes muscles to stiffen and lose flexibility. Inactivity and the aging process also contribute to this tightness. For example, you're less flexible first thing in the morning, after lying relatively still during sleep, than later in the day. As you get older, this tendency becomes more noticeable, especially if you become less active as the years pass.

So what can stretching do for you? According to Deb Merrill, a certified neuromuscular therapist in private practice in Brunswick, Maine, who has worked with Joan for several years, stretching improves flexibility, reduces muscle soreness and lessens the risk of injury from training and racing. Stretching elongates muscle fibers, relaxing the muscle and increasing your range of motion. As a runner, a greater range of motion allows you a full stride, which uses less energy and is more efficient. Increased efficiency, in turn, translates into both faster speed and fewer running injuries.

The benefits don't stop there. A good stretching session after running and racing helps flush out metabolic wastes (such as lactic acid) caught in the muscle fibers, lessening muscle soreness later. Because stretching delivers a generous supply of blood and oxygen to the depleted muscle, it relieves muscle soreness more than rest alone.

Too often, runners don't want to take the time or make the extra effort to stretch. Other priorities get in the way. But Merrill is convinced that once runners fully understand the benefits, they will be more motivated to stretch. Often, pain or injury reminds them to stretch—as it has for Joan. "My last session with Deb was overdue—I hadn't been to see her for over three weeks. Then, during a long run, I started feeling pain in my Achilles tendon, a place where I hadn't felt pain in years. After my massage session, Deb recommended several stretches to compensate for an imbalance I had developed. The fear of returning pain and tightness motivated me to keep up with the program."

Regular stretching will help keep muscles on the front, back and sides of the body equally flexible, emphasizes Merrill. Balanced in this way, flexible muscles can prevent posture problems, which can lead to muscle and joint injuries. So stretching is well worth the time it takes.

Finally, stretching expert Bob Anderson summed up the main benefit in his famous book *Stretching*. "A strong, prestretched muscle resists stress better than a strong, unstretched muscle."

When (and How) to Stretch

According to Merrill, "You should stretch every day, preferably after your workout or a warm bath, when muscles are warm and loose. If you stretch before running, warm up first by jogging lightly for at least five minutes, then stretch."

To ignore stretching is risky but improper stretching is just as bad, or worse. First of all, be sure muscles are warmed up. Stretching a cold (and shortened) muscle can put you at risk of straining that muscle, because its range of motion is restricted.

Stretching should never be painful. Pain tells you in no uncertain

DOING IT JOAN'S WAY

As you work on your stretching program, keep these handy rules in mind.

- Stretch regularly—at least three to four times per week, preferably every day.
- Hold a static stretch for at least 20 to 30 seconds.
- For best results, perform at least three sets of static stretching or 8 to 12 repetitions of active isolated (AI) stretching.
- Ease into and out of a stretch slowly.
- Stretch only warm muscles; never stretch cold muscles.
- Never bounce.
- Never stretch to the point of pain.
- Breathe naturally and stay relaxed.

terms that something is wrong—listen to it. The goal of stretching should be to develop a long, flexible muscle over time, not overnight. It takes days and weeks to get results.

Caveat: Do not stretch if you've already pulled a muscle through injury or improper stretching. In that case, Merrill suggests that massage is a safer alternative to elongate the muscle without adding stress at the weak point. But we'll talk about that shortly.

Don't Go Ballistic

You may have seen a few of them at a race or in the park: runners twisted into awkward positions, bouncing away. This method, called ballistic stretching, is no longer recommended, because it is likely to tear muscle fibers—the momentum carries the body past the normal range of motion and damages the muscle.

To understand why improper stretching that carries you past your limit is neither safe nor effective, consider how the stretch reflex works. During stretching, specialized nerves within the muscle sense when the muscle fibers are approaching their limit and signal the muscle to contract, pulling it back to protect it. Forcing the muscle beyond that limit can tear or strain the muscle. If the stretch is gradual and gentle, however, the stretch reflex kicks in, but no damage is done. Then, within 10 to 20 seconds, another impulse overrides the reflex so that it subsides, allowing further extension of the muscle. That's what makes a stretch truly beneficial.

As you stretch, keep in mind that the intensity of the stretch reflex will match the force of your stretch. So if your stretch is slow and moderate, then the contraction from the stretch reflex will be the same. But a ballistic, sudden tug on the muscle will trigger a powerful reflex action, which often tears muscle fibers.

By the way, the well-known knee-jerk reflex is an example of the stretch reflex in the upper thigh. The impact of the hammer stretches a specific muscle fiber, and the resulting jerk is its stretch-reflex response.

Three Techniques: Good, Better, Best

So much for what not to do—let's talk about three techniques that will help you stretch safely and effectively.

Static stretching. As the name implies, static stretching involves holding a position to slowly stretch the muscle. Considered the standard method, this technique is widely practiced, and Anderson literally wrote the book on it, as mentioned earlier.

How it's done: Move into your stretch until you feel a mild tension. Relax and feel the tension diminish as the stretch reflex subsides. Again, do not push to the point of pain, or even discomfort, as you can strain the muscle and cause microscopic tears in the muscle fibers.

Active isolated (AI) stretching. What if you could do an even better stretch in only two seconds? Well, you can. Aaron L. Mattes, Ph.D., a registered kinesiotherapist and licensed massage therapist in Sarasota, Florida, has developed a method that practically eliminates any possibility of injury during stretching.

Each stretch is held for two seconds, followed by a two-second rest, for 8 to 12 repetitions. To assist the stretch, you can use a towel or your hands to move into position. As with any stretch, always move slowly and gently.

AI stretching receives high marks from Merrill. "In my experience, it's by far the safest and most effective stretch. I see so many runners who don't take the time to do a static stretch properly. But when they switch to this technique, they no longer suffer muscle pulls and tears from improper stretching."

Proprioceptive neuromuscular facilitation (PNF) stretching. Your stretch can be improved noticeably in a single session of PNF, or proprioceptive neuromuscular facilitation. In PNF, a muscle contracts against some form of resistance—like a tug of war with your partner, your hands or a towel. This relaxes the muscle being stretched so that it extends into a new lengthened range. PNF is based on isometrics— the muscle contracts but doesn't actually move.

When stretching the hamstrings, for example, first move into your standing stretch position with your heel on a stair. Contract your hamstrings by pressing your heel into the stair. Relax, then contract the opposing muscle, which is the quadriceps, located on the front of the thigh, by trying to lift your heel upward. While the quadriceps is tightened, lean your upper body down into the hamstring stretch. The hamstring muscle is now stimulated to relax into a greater stretch. The end result is a more effective lengthening of the stretched muscle.

What stretching exercises are best for women who run? The

stretches in this chapter were created specifically for women runners by Merrill. Safe and effective, they combine traditional positions with improved ways of stretching.

Watch Those Hamstrings

Most runners have tight hamstrings, Merrill points out. Not surprisingly, hamstrings are the number-one site of injury she sees among her running clients. Michael Sargent, M.D., team physician at

(*continued on page 139*)

Standing hamstring muscle stretch. Stand with one leg extended and resting on a step or bench, below waist level. (The second or third stair on a staircase is optimum height.) This leg should be straight but not locked at the knee. Bend your supporting leg slightly, with the foot pointing forward. First, contract your hamstrings briefly by pushing your heel down into the stair. Relax, then tighten the front of the thigh (quadriceps muscle) of your extended leg as you lean forward from the lower back, as if to lift your foot off the stair. Bring your upper body closer to your leg until you feel the stretch of the hamstring muscle along the back of your thigh. Hold for two seconds then release for two seconds. Repeat ten times. Repeat with the opposite leg.

Be careful to lean with your entire upper body, not just your head and shoulders. Bend from your hip and lower your chest toward your knee. Keep your lower back flat, not rounded over.

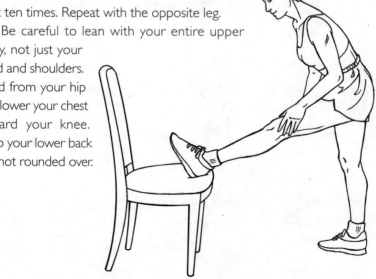

Raised-leg hamstring muscle stretch. Lie on your back. Extend one leg straight out and raise the other. Using both hands, grasp the raised leg as close to the ankle as possible and pull your shin toward your nose. In this exercise, the knee is bent slightly (designed for those with less flexibility) to focus the stretch on the middle of the muscle. Don't worry if your hip or head rises off the ground. Hold for two seconds then release. Repeat ten times. Repeat with the opposite leg.

For PNF resistance (see page 132), push the leg away from your body and into your hands for two seconds, then pull the leg toward you to stretch the hamstring. Repeat ten times. Your head and buttocks may rise off the floor while doing this push-pull, and your opposite leg may bend slightly.

Standing calf muscle stretch. Facing a wall, stand two to three feet away, placing one foot about two feet behind the other. Press against the wall with your hands, keeping your forward knee bent and back knee straight, with both heels on the ground. Keeping your back straight, slowly move your chest toward the wall for two seconds, then back off for two seconds. Repeat ten times. This stretches the large calf muscle at the back of the leg (gastrocnemius). For PNF resistance (see page 132), lift the toes of the back foot during the stretch.

Variation: To include the inner calf muscle (soleus) in the stretch, bend the knee of the back leg and stretch it toward the floor for an additional two seconds—for a total of four seconds. Release for two seconds, as before. Switch legs and alternate with the straight leg stretch. Repeat both stretches ten times each.

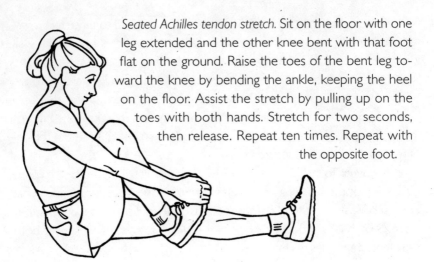

Seated Achilles tendon stretch. Sit on the floor with one leg extended and the other knee bent with that foot flat on the ground. Raise the toes of the bent leg toward the knee by bending the ankle, keeping the heel on the floor. Assist the stretch by pulling up on the toes with both hands. Stretch for two seconds, then release. Repeat ten times. Repeat with the opposite foot.

Inner thigh and groin stretch. Sit on the floor with your knees bent and the soles of your feet touching. Your knees should be projected to the sides. Relaxing your inner thigh muscles, lower your knees toward the floor as far as possible, then press down on your knees gently with your hands for two seconds. Release and repeat ten times.

To increase the stretch even further, grasp your ankles with your hands, lean forward and gently press against your knees with your elbows. Take care not to pull your toes upward.

For PNF resistance (see page 132), push your knees up against your elbows for two seconds, then stretch down. Repeat ten times.

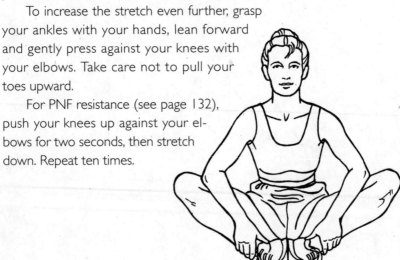

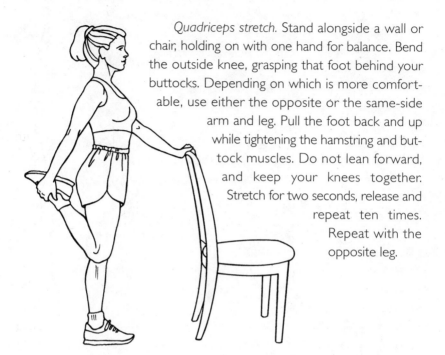

Quadriceps stretch. Stand alongside a wall or chair, holding on with one hand for balance. Bend the outside knee, grasping that foot behind your buttocks. Depending on which is more comfortable, use either the opposite or the same-side arm and leg. Pull the foot back and up while tightening the hamstring and buttock muscles. Do not lean forward, and keep your knees together. Stretch for two seconds, release and repeat ten times. Repeat with the opposite leg.

Lower back stretch (spinal twist). Sit on the floor with your right leg straight and your left leg bent. Cross the left foot over the right leg, placing it alongside the right knee. Place your right elbow on the outside of your left leg, near your knee. Slowly turn your head and upper body toward the left. Gently press your elbow outward against your bent leg toward the right side of your body. You should feel the stretch in your lower back and on the side of your hip. Hold for two seconds and relax for two seconds. Repeat ten times. Change sides and repeat.

Biceps and chest stretch. Stand with your feet shoulder-width apart, knees slightly bent and arms extended straight back. Interlace your fingers behind your lower back, keeping your elbows straight. Squeeze your shoulder blades together in the back and lift your hands upward behind you. Do not lean forward. Hold for two seconds, relax for two seconds and repeat ten times.

Triceps stretch. To stretch the triceps muscle at the back of the upper arm, bend the arm and place that hand behind your head so that it rests between your shoulder blades at the top of your back. With the opposite hand on the bent elbow, gently assist the stretch, pulling up on the bent elbow for two seconds. Release for two seconds and repeat ten times. Repeat with the other arm.

the University of Vermont in Burlington, explains, "Tightness in the hamstrings results because the muscles span two joints, the hip and the knee. During running, the upper portion contracts as the hamstrings extend the hip to propel you forward, but the lower portion must simultaneously relax as the knee is extended. No wonder they often protest."

Caution: When stretching the hamstrings, you should feel this stretch in the belly of the muscle (in the middle of the back of your thigh). If you feel a sharp pain under your buttocks or your knee, you may have some muscle or tendon damage, and you should ease up on this stretch. Continue with other stretching and give this area time to heal.

If It Hurts, Rub It

As mentioned earlier, massage can be a valuable preventive measure in avoiding injuries. And it makes sense. Rubbing a muscle that hurts is a normal response. Along with stretching, massage helps to increase circulation and thus rejuvenate a muscle. Massage assists recovery between training sessions, which improves athletic performance and endurance. By helping to detect stress and muscular imbalances, massage can prevent injuries. It also helps recuperation by restoring mobility to injured muscle tissue.

"Massage and stretching help to reverse the spasms that can result from fatigue, strain or postworkout soreness," Dr. Sargent points out. Many runners and other athletes benefit from regular massages done by qualified professionals.

Every one to two weeks, depending on her training load, Joan gets a one-hour neuromuscular massage that includes sports massage along with triggerpoint therapy and other specialized techniques effective for athletes. She has been using different forms of massage since the early 1980s and has found it very therapeutic.

Your First Massage

Massage can make your body feel great, but it is more than an indulgence; it is an important part of training. If you are contemplating getting your first massage, do it at least three days before a race. Most people feel drained or too relaxed afterward to be ready for a race effort.

For some people, a massage—particularly the first one—can result in some muscle soreness from the natural waste products of metabolism being released from tight muscle fibers. Triggerpoint therapy, for example, releases metabolic wastes trapped in the contracted muscle "knots." Drinking enough fluids (eight glasses of water a day) after receiving deep muscle work becomes even more important so that wastes can be flushed out of the system.

Self-Massage—The Gift You Give Yourself

Massage doesn't necessarily require an appointment and a fee. You can also do some easy self-massage or share the work with partner massage.

Squeeze, use friction and massage the muscle with your knuckles, thumbs and hands. Use smooth strokes, lifting, squeezing and compressing with the hands. You can also roll the skin or use rapid friction. Other tools of self-massage include rolling a tennis ball on the buttocks or on the lower back (while standing with your back against the ball on a wall) or using a rolling pin on the calves or thighs.

Before you start, make sure you can wiggle the muscle around. Do not work on tense or contracted muscles. The muscle should be limp and relaxed, not elongated in a stretched position. You can't properly massage the Achilles tendons or calves while standing up, for example. Sit down and cross your leg over your knee to make sure the area is relaxed.

Using cream or oil, knead and massage the general area to soften it. Squeeze the muscles, make deep circles with your fingers or thumbs and pull long strokes toward your torso (and your heart). In the process, you will usually find the origin of your pain, and you can work on the area more deeply and specifically.

For painful areas, use the triggerpoint technique. Press the tender spot gently for ten seconds, then release. If the pain or tightness does not subside, wait about five minutes and then repeat for another ten seconds using less pressure. This technique can be difficult to perform if the area is very tender. As Joan explains, "I need a partner to maintain the pressure. I tend to let up too quickly when it's sensitive."

Good areas to massage are the calves, hamstrings and inner and outer thighs. Concentrate also on the buttocks, as women runners

tend to have more tightness in this area. You can do self-massage before a run to loosen up, but make it a light massage. In general, whenever you practice self-massage, spend no more than ten minutes on
any given area. Otherwise, you may bruise yourself. In addition, you
don't want to work hard over bones or on top of bony protuberances
like kneecaps.

NEUROMUSCULAR THERAPY: TEACH YOUR MUSCLES TO RELAX

As a cutting-edge approach to the management of running
injuries, neuromuscular therapy relieves pain and improves gait,
posture and muscle balance by "teaching" muscles how to stretch
and relax.

Tight muscles and numerous injuries prompted Joan to seek
out a therapist who could do regular body work on her that was
both healing and rejuvenative. Her search led to Deb Merrill, a
certified neuromuscular therapist in private practice in Brunswick,
Maine. Merrill has worked with Joan extensively since 1990, and
Joan credits her with helping to relieve her chronic lower back and
hip problems.

As Merrill explains it, "By manipulating muscles, tendons, ligaments and fascia, muscles are re-educated to release tension and
stay relaxed all the time." Along with postural analysis, gait biomechanics analysis, assisted stretching and self-care techniques, treatments include manual manipulation, in which muscles are stretched
and compressed without harmful consequences.

When Merrill treats Joan, she assesses her alignment and as-
signs specific stretches to counter certain imbalances Joan tends to
develop when she trains heavily. In this way, each session provides
preventive care as well as an active form of accelerated healing. So
for runners like Joan, NMT serves as an alternative to the traditional routes of medication, surgery or waiting it out.

CHAPTER 11

CROSS-TRAINING AND DRILLS

Whole-Body Benefits

In the 1984 Olympic Marathon, Joan needed tremendous stamina to withstand the heat and the competition and to go on to win. Having had knee surgery just 17 days prior to the Olympic trials, she was faced with the dilemma of training for the biggest race of her life while allowing her knee to heal. Her solution was cross-training. Stationary cycling and swimming enabled Joan to maintain pre-injury levels of strength and endurance that she needed to win the marathon despite her knee injury.

What Variety Can Do for You

Cross-training first became popular with the emergence of the triathlon, a combination swim, bike and run event at its height in the 1980s. But cross-training—which involves doing two or more fitness activities or sports—can include almost any combination of sports. Why cross-train? For so many reasons.

Strength and fitness. Cross-training will help you achieve a higher level of overall fitness than sticking to a single activity. No one sport can work all muscles equally, but by alternating between two or more activities, you can optimize your conditioning.

As a runner, you can use cross-training to develop and strengthen muscles that running doesn't exercise. Rowing, for example, will develop upper body strength, which in turn can further enhance running efficiency. As a supplement, cross-training can improve or maintain a runner's cardiovascular endurance, provided the alternative training imposes comparable physical demands.

Injury prevention and recovery. Because cross-training allows you to rest one set of muscles while working another, you are less likely to wear down the same muscle group day after day, which can lead to injury. Thus, balancing running with swimming, for example, reduces the natural risks of continually stressing the legs and feet from the impact of running.

Since Joan follows a fairly heavy running schedule, she doesn't ordinarily use other activities to train. But cross-training speeds healing by increasing circulation and maintaining range of motion. "I tend to depend on cross-training when I'm injured and can't run. Although I pursue many other sports and activities for recreation when I'm healthy, I participate just for fun."

In fact, at times, Joan has gotten hooked on her cross-training. "When I had my Achilles tendon surgery, I was forced to swim and bike instead of run. I got into such a routine that when I was told it was okay to go back to running, I was a bit reluctant to leave the other activities behind. It proved to me that I could find satisfaction and benefits in other training activities besides running.

"Perhaps if I cross-trained on a regular basis, I wouldn't get injured," concludes Joan. Her advice is to not wait until you get injured to cross-train; take up at least one alternative sport while you're healthy.

Balance and variety. Cross-training activities invariably tax different muscles than those used in running. As these muscles are strengthened, a more balanced, overall fitness results. Without a doubt, Joan understands this balance and variety. "I believe I am a strong runner—physically and mentally—partly because I had a varied sports background. I had the opportunity to compete in such sports as skiing, tennis, field hockey, basketball and softball. I gained different benefits from each of these sports, even though I might not have excelled in all of them."

Variety not only develops your athleticism, but it helps prevent boredom or staleness. Says Joan, "Cross-training can also give you a mental edge and keep you psychologically fresh. Plus, it teaches you a lot about your strengths and weaknesses, helps you improve as a runner and builds confidence."

And, of course, indoor workouts of some kind help you stay in shape when the weather is too hot or the roads are too icy to run effectively or safely.

Planning Your Program

If you're ready to cross-train, the list of possibilities is endless: swimming, bicycling, aerobics, step classes, water running.... Joan says, "Think about what you want to get out of it. Are you looking for a little variety to cut boredom? Then pick an activity just for fun, like

CHILD CARE AS CROSS-TRAINING

Joan counts pushing, pulling and carrying children, as well as her household tasks, as part of her fitness routine. She also includes such tasks as stacking and carrying wood and a substantial amount of gardening and yardwork.

You don't have to chop wood, though. If you live a city life, look for ways to incorporate more physical activity or exercise into your daily routine. Try power walking or cycling for transportation, use stairs whenever possible in your office or apartment building or turn on the music and dance or skip rope—with children or without. If you use your imagination, there's no limit to these added extras.

in-line skating. Are you trying to achieve more balanced fitness as a runner? Then you might want to develop your upper body with rowing. If you're feeling some early shin pain, biking could be a good alternate to take the stress off of your legs while still conditioning them and without losing endurance. I even know some runners who swear by yoga or karate. Surprisingly, many women try boxing. Find the activity that is most convenient, enjoyable and valuable to you. Experiment."

There's no one right way to cross-train. In order to improve your running, you could choose activities that build leg strength and endurance, such as bicycling, step classes, cross-country skiing or water running. Otherwise, your choice depends on your lifestyle, fitness needs, talents, finances, time schedule and, above all, what you like. Do you prefer to work out indoors or outdoors? Alone or with others? Are you willing to pay for a gym membership or equipment? Do you have the time to devote to scheduled or team activities, or is a home-based program—such as free weights or exercise videos—best for you?

Is there a limit to how much cross-training you should do? It depends on your current workout schedule and what you're used to. You may not be as good at a new activity as you are at running—at least not at first. Work out until you feel you have duplicated your running effort, if a substitute session is your goal. Or, try to work out for the same amount of time as you run. If you want to be more scientific, use heart rate as a guide and match the effort.

If you're looking to invest in a piece of exercise equipment, Joan suggests something new or different. "If you run, consider a rowing machine or stair climber. I'm not an experienced stair climber, but I like the intensity of the workout, which builds up the leg muscles and pushes endurance. If I had to do it over, I would have bought a stair climber instead of my treadmill."

If you're taking up a technique sport for the first time, lessons are a good investment, and they aren't always expensive. If you've joined a health club, for example, instruction in all activities is usually included in your membership. For other sports, a half-day of instruction can give you a head start on mastering the form.

Running in Place: Treadmill Training

Joan positions her treadmill in front of a large picture window in her living room. The view is pretty, but she'd be happier to have the company in a health club. Instead, she listens to music. (It's the only time she feels the need for a distraction to help her through a workout.)

"I'm most apt to use my treadmill in the winter," says Joan. "It helps to be able to run without being distracted by weather or poor road conditions." She also feels that, for her at least, running on a treadmill powered by a motor and using a programmed pace encourages her not only to vary the pace and alter the incline but to stick to that pace. Although there are some lower-impact models available, Joan's only caution is that many treadmill surfaces tend to be hard, so you should give yourself time to adapt gradually to the new surface.

Going in Cycles: Bicycling

Whether outside on the roads and trails or indoors on a stationary bike, bicycling is a popular activity among runners. Mountain or trail biking, a more rugged ride done on bikes with softer, wider tires, is soaring in popularity. And a fit biker can make a nice trip out of a cycling session, turning training into an enjoyable social event.

Make sure your bike is properly fitted, with the correct distance between seat and pedal. Getting the right fit is critical to prevent back and arm strain. "Your knee should be slightly bent when the pedal is at the bottom," stresses Joan. As a runner, she gets a better workout by cycling in a higher gear as opposed to a lower one, so she isn't pedaling with as many revolutions but the resistance is higher per stroke. Joan feels that a higher number of revolutions puts her at risk for knee trouble. On the other hand, she cautions not to make the gear so high that the knee joint is stressed while pedaling.

Fluid Movement: Swimming

Swimming offers a welcome respite from any stress caused by land sports like running. The water supports and relaxes the body, and swimming is generally injury-free. Joan ranks swimming high on her list of cross-training activities, especially for postmarathon training when her legs need a rest from impact. She feels swimming is particularly beneficial for certain knee, ankle or foot injuries. Also, she adds, for the runner with tight muscles, swimming provides some flexibility.

When you first switch from a sport at which you are adept, like running, to one at which you are not, your technique may be a bit awkward. "When I started swimming, I tried to spend as much time in the pool as I did running. But I had to work on my technique before my workouts became equally effective. It took considerable effort to overcome inefficiency at first, but that effort can be part of the workout as well."

Once she became adept, Joan worked on both endurance and interval swimming, and her lap workouts began to feel similar to track workouts.

Reaching Out: Rowing

Joan has tried rowing and testifies that it builds great cardiovascular fitness and strengthens the abdominals, arms and upper back—parts of the body running doesn't address. Just in case you don't happen to live on the Charles River and own your own personal sculling craft, portable home rowing machines fill the bill. Joan also suggests kayaking or canoeing, too, if you get the chance.

Rolling Along: In-Line Skating

This is a great way to develop your legs and have fun at the same time. This high-tech version of a childhood game provides a moderately good cardiovascular workout (which increases with faster, harder skating). Joan skates on her running routes, sometimes while she pushes her children in a stroller.

Going Deep: Water Running

Runners love this fast-growing exercise because they can duplicate the effort of running—from easy jog to intervals—minus the impact. Like swimming, water running is great during injury recovery and for postmarathon workouts.

Water running classes are popping up everywhere, but you can try it on your own. Buy an inexpensive flotation belt (or vest or other device) and head for water deep enough so that your feet don't touch the bottom.

Joan has had some excellent workouts with water running. "On and off throughout the 1980s, I used water running for injury recovery and during pregnancy. After only one week, I felt I was getting the same results in the pool as I did on the roads." For some sessions, Joan blended two activities, swimming for a half-hour (for a warm-up) and then water running.

Gliding Along: Skiing

Between downhill skiing and cross-country skiing, Joan spends nearly every winter weekend on the trails. "Cross-country skiing is probably the best possible supplemental training for a runner; fantastic training for the legs as well as the upper body, and it gives an excellent cardiovascular workout," says Joan. But Joan lives in Maine. If snow is rare in your part of the country, you can still train on a cross-country ski machine.

Test Your Mettle: Strength Training

Runners frequently want to know if strength training can make them better runners. With more and more women picking up barbells, women runners ask the same question.

Joan Samuelson believes in strength training, which she does mostly during her off-season from competition. "It is particularly important for me to work my upper body, which is understandably much weaker than my lower body. My arms look like chicken wings in relation to my thighs, which have always been big, starting with my early skiing days." As she explains, "It stands to reason that the better you balance the strength of your upper and lower body, the more efficient, and thus faster, a runner you will be."

In addition to building up weaker areas of the body, strength training improves overall body shape and appearance. Nothing tones muscles like strength training.

Resistance training is of particular importance to two specific groups of runners: women who are new to sports and those who are over 40 years of age.

In the case of both men and women masters runners (over 40), strength training is instrumental to counter the natural increase in body fat with age as well as the potential decrease in bone strength. It also builds more muscle mass, which burns more calories than fat, even at rest, because it is metabolically more active.

Rules of Resistance

"Strength training provides another type of body awareness for women, even simply going through the body's full range of motion, which may not occur with other sports," says Ramona Melvin, a personal trainer and fitness expert at Equinox Health Club in New York City. Here, Melvin gives her rules and guidelines for strengthening the body by working against resistance.

Follow the basics. The principles of strength training are the same as for stretching, speed work or any physical activity. Do it after a warm-up, when muscles are more elastic and efficient. Muscles well-supplied with blood ensure optimum range of motion and less likelihood of injury.

Work opposing sets of muscles. After working the quadriceps at the front of the thigh, for example, work the hamstrings in the back next. This balances them by allowing one set of muscles to stretch out while the other group is being worked.

Always start with the largest muscle groups. First of all, this serves to warm up the entire body for the workout, and second, if you exercise the small muscle groups first, you may fatigue them to the point that the larger groups will not get as good a workout. If you tire the biceps or triceps in the arms, for example, your back will not fully benefit if the arms have become too tired to give full strength or range of motion during the back exercises.

Work at a slow and steady pace. Pick a consistent but relatively slow, controlled speed at which to move through your exercises, and stay with that pace. The negative portion of the movement, when the weight is lowered, should be done just as slowly as the lifting portion.

Melvin warns against speeding up the last few repetitions or at the end point of a repetition. "Do not pop and drop," as she puts it, "but control the movement in both directions." Think of squeezing the muscles as you do the exercise to keep the movement smooth and controlled.

Do not lock the joints. You can get the proper extension and full range of motion without locking joints like knees and elbows, which is especially risky when the weight is directly loaded on the joint. Practice feeling the difference between extension and lock without weight before trying the exercise.

Don't train with pain. It's important to fully understand the difference between pain and fatigue. Do not work into the pain zone. Doing the exercises will help you understand the particular level of fatigue you will undergo. The workout should be tiring, not painful.

Use common sense. If any strength training exercises aggravate a pre-existing condition (such as back or knee strain), cut back in intensity and/or range of motion, or drop the exercise altogether.

Stay in good form. Practice good posture alignment and proper form for all exercises. Melvin is adamant about this. "The moment fatigue disturbs proper form, stop the exercise," she says.

Breathe with the movement. Breathing plays a key role in strength training. Concentrate on exhaling forcefully during the effort and inhaling during the negative segment of the exercise, when the weight is lowered. This rhythm synchronizes the muscle contraction with the diaphragm, which contracts as you inhale.

Save your running shoes. If you want to protect your running shoes from excess wear, do not use them for strength training. Melvin claims moves such as lunges can stretch the toe box, and loading weight will break down the midsole. Use cross-training shoes or old running shoes, so long as they are not so worn that they no longer provide support and stability.

Start light. It's always wise to start conservatively with the lightest weights. As you improve, you can upgrade and add to your equipment. For any beginning program, develop proper form first by performing exercises without weights.

Know when to skip it. Competitive runners do not generally weight train during their racing season, when it would drain them, but year-round road runners may continue throughout the year, taking occasional breaks during critical times such as the week of a race. In addition, some runners omit lower-body exercises altogether, as they feel it is an added stress with running.

Be consistent. Train a minimum of twice a week, preferably three times, depending on how much you run. Remember, something is always better than nothing, and consistency will develop the habit.

Drills for Better Running

Basketball players, sprinters and now you—you all have something in common. These drills! By doing them routinely, you'll build both strength and agility, which can dramatically help your running performance.

Joan is a strong advocate of drills. "Drills are good for conditioning during build-up phases of training and while coming back from injury. They help to balance the 'super powers' (the legs) of the runner's body by strengthening individual weak areas." For variety and overall development as an athlete, a runner might skip running one day each week and substitute a workout of drills and strength training. Joan advises that "to do these drills properly, stay focused and give them 100 percent of your concentration."

John Babington, coach at the Liberty Athletic Club for 19 years and assistant coach for the 1996 Olympic women's track-and-field team, explains, "these drills are designed to take you through the running stride methodically and progressively," to help runners gain an appreciation of what he calls the simple but complicated act of running.

"To be convinced of their benefit, just look at the average runner," notes Babington. "Many people seem tight and inflexible, clearly not going through the entire range of motion. That's why they have a shuffling gait."

Babington began prescribing these drills over a decade ago. His first athlete to use them, 1500-meter runner and Harvard University all-American Darlene Beckford, made her breakthrough performances shortly afterward. Olympic medalist Lynn Jennings used these drills to prepare for the 1992 Olympic Games. "She achieved her best running mechanics ever," says Babington, "which allowed her to run a rigorous program of heats and a final, in spikes, without her form getting ragged."

Following the principle of progression, the first four drills are fairly mild, proceeding to more strenuous sets of drills. The drills use all muscles and joints engaged in the running motion as well as those that support the running motion.

These drills can be done as a workout by themselves, as part of a warm-up procedure for a run or after a moderate run. If done as a separate workout, always warm up first by running one to two miles, then include stretching. As part of a running warm-up, include as few or as many drills as you like. Test combinations to see what blends best with your running, but Babington suggests using Walking on Balls of Feet, Jogging Elastically, Heeling and High Skipping (see below).

Babington also suggests doing a few favorite drills before speed work or a race as part of the warm-up. "They wake up various muscles," he explains, "and I tell my athletes that using them before a race can intimidate the opposition."

Do these drills on a smooth surface and, preferably, a soft one. The distance for each drill is indicated, but if form deteriorates, shorten the drill segments to a more comfortable length. Specifically, for Marching and High Knee Lifts, you can shorten them to 2 × 50 meters. With any other drills, you can shorten them to 1 × 100 meters or 2 × 50 meters.

Walking on Balls of Feet I

Muscles worked: calves and feet.

Distance: 2 × 100 meters.

Walk forward with a slow cadence. With your heels striking first, rise markedly up on the balls of your feet. Hold the arms in running position (see page 126) and keep them relaxed.

Walking on Balls of Feet II

Muscles worked: hip flexors (top and front part of the thighs), calves and feet; also promotes proper running posture.

Distance: 2 × 100 meters.

Clasp your hands behind your head, elbows straight out to the sides. Taking slightly elongated strides, walk forward, heels striking first, then step onto the balls of your feet. Allow a brief pause before beginning each step. As you walk, feel the extension and stretch in the hip flexor of your back leg. If you do not feel a stretch, try taking slightly longer steps.

Walking on Balls of Feet III

Muscles worked: hip flexors, calves and feet; also promotes proper running posture.

Distance: 2 × 100 meters.

Use the same technique as Walking on Balls of Feet II but walk with your hands straight overhead, reaching for the sky. The hips should be high and forward (the pelvis tipped forward). Emphasize slight overstriding, while reaching as high as possible with each step.

Jogging Elastically

Muscles worked: calves (more actively than Walking on Balls of Feet I).

Distance: 4 × 100 meters.

This looks like a jog without the heels touching the ground. Staying entirely on the balls of your feet, jog forward slowly. Try to feel as if you are supporting your weight "elastically," like a rubber band.

Minibounding

Muscles worked: all muscles of the lower legs that support the body and propel it forward during running.

Distance: 2 × 100 meters.

Exaggerating the form of Jogging Elastically, jog forward while forcefully pushing off by flexing the calf muscle and extending the ankle joint. Keep the arms in running position. Try doing this drill with a wider stance, placing your feet about 18 inches apart to the sides. Do not overstride—these are fairly short bounds.

Heeling

Muscles worked: hamstrings; also improves range of motion.

Distance: 4 × 100 meters.

In a fairly rapid tempo, jog forward by lightly kicking your buttocks with your heels. Keep your arms relaxed, in running position. Keep your posture straight and use minimal knee lift and pushoff. You should barely move forward.

Marching

Muscles worked: hip flexors; also increases range of motion.
Distance: 2 × 100 meters.

Take quick steps, lifting your knees as high as possible. Move forward slowly. Focus on the height of the step. Do not overstride. Hold the arms in running position. Use them to help lift the knees. Your opposite hand and leg should be lifted simultaneously. Try to lift your leg so that the upper leg is parallel to the ground.

High Knee Lifts

Muscles worked: hip flexors.
Distance: 2 × 100 meters.

This drill is done like Marching but while running instead of walking. Take quick walking steps, lifting your knees as high as possible. Move forward slowly. Focus on the height of the step. Do not overstride. Hold the arms in running position. Use them to help lift the knees. Your opposite hand and leg should be lifted simultaneously. Try to lift your leg so that the upper leg is parallel to the ground.

Skipping

Muscles worked: all the muscles used in previous drills.
Distance: 2 × 100 meters.

Think of being a child again. Skip in a smooth, relaxed and effortless fashion. This drill gets you into a rhythm for High Skipping and relaxes the body.

High Skipping

Muscles worked: all the muscles used in previous drills, taking them through their entire running range of motion.
Distance: 2 × 100 meters.

Skip as above but concentrate on simultaneously driving the up-lifted knee with the opposite arm. Push off vigorously. You should not move forward at a fast rate. Equal emphasis should be given to the pushoff from the back leg and the drive upward of the free leg. Try to lift your leg so that the upper leg is parallel to the ground.

PART III

THE WINNING
EDGE

CHAPTER 12

EATING FOR OPTIMUM ENERGY

A Woman Runner's Nutritional Needs

As a woman, your nutritional needs are different from a man's. If you're a woman runner, you have additional needs created by athletic effort. But don't assume that, as a woman runner and serious athlete, Joan follows a diet of energy bars washed down with sports drinks interspersed with major episodes of carbo loading. Joan is a real person with a real family who eats real food. And that's as it should be. The optimal diet for women runners, be they recreational runners or elite champions, is rooted in good, well-grounded basics, centering around the three major components of food—carbohydrates, protein and fats—and water, perhaps the most critically important nutrient of all.

In general, meals should combine a high proportion of carbohydrates, which provide ready energy and fuel the muscles, a lower ration of protein (to help build and repair the body) and a modest amount of fat, a highly concentrated form of energy. The recommended proportions break down as follows:

60 to 70 percent carbohydrates

15 to 20 percent protein

20 to 25 percent fat

This breakdown, with such a heavy emphasis on carbohydrates, was once mainly the diet for endurance athletes like marathoners. But it has since become the prescription for a healthy diet for the general population. Nancy Clark, R.D., noted nutrition author and nutritional consultant at Sportsmedicine in Brookline, Massachusetts, confirms this: "Both couch potatoes and runners alike should eat a high-carbohydrate, moderate-protein, low-fat diet. This will fuel the muscles and invest in better health."

The body needs about 40 vitamins and minerals. Think of these nutrients as the spark plugs that keep your engine running smoothly. And keep in mind that the greater the variety of foods, the greater the number of nutrients.

Active Women: Now Hear This

What you eat before a workout should fuel you but not impede your effort. If you eat before exercise, give yourself enough time (one hour for a snack, three hours for a full meal) to digest your food. And if you're going to run hard, allow even more time.

Choose easily digestible pre-run meals of high-starch, low-fat foods like breads and pastas. If you have problems eating before a run, especially before a race, try semisoft foods such as oatmeal, yogurt or even juice.

Many runners prefer not to eat before a race if they are nervous for fear it will hamper their performance. For a long distance, such as the marathon, it's good to have at least something simple like toast or a bagel a couple of hours before the race. And make sure to eat well the night before and afterward.

What you eat after a long or strenuous effort, like a race or hard workout, is as important as what you eat before—a fact many runners often don't adequately consider. After a marathon, for example, replenishing muscle glycogen (fuel stores) can affect your recovery.

Initially, after any hard effort, be sure to drink plenty of water. You may also want an electrolyte-replacement drink, a glass of juice or some other carbohydrate, followed by a moderate, carbohydrate-rich meal within two hours, such as two slices of bread and juice or a bowl of cereal with fruit.

What about sports bars? Compact and lightweight, these vitamin-enriched bars are very handy, but you pay for that convenience. Are they worth it? As Clark points out, these bars do give you an energy boost, but low-fat granola bars or fig bars from the supermarket can also provide quick energy at a fraction of the cost. "In fact," she concludes, "a handful of raisins can do a great job, with no fat, at a very low price."

Water, Water Everywhere

You'll see it at races—start, finish and in the middle—yet even serious runners can fail to realize the importance of enough drinking water or other fluids during exercise. That's because the thirst mechanism is not an accurate gauge of your fluid needs. So, from the easiest to the toughest exercise, don't wait to feel thirsty—drink.

On a warm day, you should drink one or two cups of water before training and another cup every 15 to 20 minutes while running. Don't forget to continue to drink after a workout as well. Watery foods—such as salads and fruits—also help hydrate and replace electrolytes such as potassium.

When it's cold, you may not notice dehydration as much, but you still lose considerable amounts of water. Watch out for symptoms such as a headache, muscle cramps, light-headedness and general fatigue.

Not only can dehydration affect running performance, it can cause serious health problems like heatstroke, cramps and exhaustion. In some extreme cases, heat illness can be fatal. So drink before you feel thirsty or show signs of dehydration.

If you prefer sports drinks, drink them if you like the taste, but experts say you probably don't need them for workouts less than an hour. Joan prefers water or juice after her training runs—lemonade is her favorite refresher when at home. At races, she's happy to accept the sports drinks that are offered. "Before a marathon, like Boston, I've usually been sipping water throughout the morning. During the race, I think sports drinks help me avoid dehydration and depletion, and even high-energy bars serve a purpose, although I usually eat them after, not during, the race."

Water does the trick for all but intense, prolonged exercise. There's only a minor loss through sweat of electrolytes and minerals—which many sports drinks aim to replace. For longer sessions, however, some studies indicate that carbohydrate solutions may furnish energy during the effort. Test any drink in training before trying it in a race in the event it causes gastrointestinal distress for you.

Another type of sports drink is designed for carbohydrate replacement to refuel exercised muscles immediately after a workout. If you're not inclined to eat afterward, a carbohydrate drink can be useful. It also provides calories and, therefore, energy. But beware— these drinks alone do not substitute for wholesome foods.

Making the Best Food Choices

Of course, good nutrition for women runners isn't linked only to performance-related guidelines. What you eat on a day-to-day basis is equally important. Nutrient-dense foods pack the biggest nutritional punch per calorie, and here's the best of the bunch, based on rankings by the Center for Science in the Public Interest, located in Washington, D.C., and its publication "Nutrition Action Newsletter."

Vegetables. When choosing vegetables, think dark and colorful. Tomatoes, green peppers (sweet red peppers are even better), carrots and dark leafy vegetables far surpass the nutritional quality of pale iceberg lettuce, cucumbers, onions, celery and radishes. Asparagus, peas, winter squash and pumpkin add color, flavor and nutrition to any meal. Pick broccoli over green beans, potatoes over corn, kale and yams over almost anything. Generally, fresh vegetables hold the most nutritional value but frozen can be as good (and sometimes better). Choose both over canned vegetables.

Joan's large garden provides her with the freshest vegetables, and the ritual of growing them is "very therapeutic and rewarding." In fact, she traditionally plants her first seeds of the season the week before the Boston Marathon.

While gardening is a pleasurable complement to her running, Joan warns all runners to "watch your gardening posture and technique. Holding awkward positions or staying in the same position for long periods can leave you very sore and tight the next day."

Fruit. Who doesn't love the taste of fruit? And juices are great right after exercise for replacing water and minerals like potassium and magnesium. Make your optimum choices; choose papaya, cantaloupe, strawberries, oranges, tangerines, bananas and apricots over green grapes, pears, plums and apples. Overall, the mango is a real winner. And dried fruits, like figs and prunes, supply iron, fiber and potassium.

Meats and fish. Look for lean cuts of meat, as animal fats are saturated and contain cholesterol. Chicken and turkey are usually lower in fat than red meats. When buying ground meat, turkey breast is significantly leaner than beef or turkey made from parts, which often includes skin that is high in fat.

Fish, a great source of protein and generally low in fat if not fried, is renowned for its heart-healthy omega-3 fatty acids, components of a polyunsaturated fat found in some fish oils. According to Clark, not all fish are high in omega-3's, but some good sources are Atlantic mackerel, king mackerel, Pacific herring and lake trout.

Cereals and grains. Whole grains and flours, as in bran cereals and dark breads, supply more nutrition than foods made with refined or white flour. Among other grains, try experimenting with the top-rated quinoa, amaranth, buckwheat groats, bulgur and pearled barley over corn grits, soba noodles, couscous and instant or converted white rice.

Choose low-fat crackers, breads and muffins. If reading labels for fat content doesn't give you a clue (one serving of about 100 calories should be under three grams of fat), place the cracker or muffin on a paper napkin. If it leaves a grease stain, it's high in fat and you should eat it in moderation.

Beans. Beans are a nutritional powerhouse, and those at the very top of the list include soybeans, pinto beans, chick-peas (garbanzos and ceci) and lentils.

Can Supplements Help?

It's best to get nutrients from food, says Clark. Don't substitute vitamin and mineral supplements for healthy eating. A great percentage of women, however—runners among them—do take iron or calcium supplements, along with a balanced diet, to ensure they are meeting their needs.

If you are among those who do take supplements, keep in mind the following tips. Choose calcium lactate, calcium gluconate or calcium carbonate but not supplements made from bonemeal, dolomite or oyster shells, which have been found to contain lead. Try not to combine calcium and iron in the same meal, since calcium may hamper the absorption of iron. Take both calcium and iron supplements with a source of vitamin C, such as orange juice, to enhance absorption.

Many experts believe that most people, whether active or not, don't eat balanced diets, and, therefore, they recommend a daily multivitamin. Depending on her needs, Joan has supplemented her diet with a multivitamin as well as vitamins C, E and B complex. "At certain times, like when I was pregnant or nursing or during a stressful period in my life, I feel my need for these vitamins is higher."

Vitamins C and E, along with beta-carotene, are antioxidants; that is, they prevent damage to cells from oxidation, a process not unlike the destruction of metals by rust. Antioxidants have been shown to help prevent certain cancers and heart disease. Because antioxidants may help prevent muscle damage and promote muscle recovery, some researchers recommend that active exercisers increase their intake. In addition, vitamin C helps the body cope with physical stress, which can lead to fatigue, and vitamin E helps deliver more oxygen to tissues. Both of these are valuable benefits to runners.

Traditional Taboos

Should you avoid all foods with salt and sugar if you want to follow a healthy diet? Or abstain from alcohol and caffeine to perform well as a runner? Not necessarily. Clark assures, "There's room in a good diet for some of the 'forbidden foods.' And what's more, absolute deprivation can backfire."

Sugar. In a balanced diet, up to 10 percent of calories can come from refined sugar, believes Clark. That's about 200 calories (12 teaspoons of sugar or one can of soda and a cookie) for an active woman who eats about 2,000 calories per day. "The sugar fuels your muscles and can be a tasty addition to your sports diet," says Clark.

Joan enjoys sweets and is an adept baker. Because she prepares her own baked goods, she knows exactly what's in them. "I usually cut down by one-half to two-thirds the amount of sugar a recipe calls for and cut the butter or margarine by half as well. Replacing the fat with an equal amount of pureed or mashed fruit (banana or apple) keeps the food moist and sweet. I use unbleached flour or a portion of whole-wheat flour, wheat germ or rolled oats. Recently, I have been using canola and safflower oil in recipes. I have even used olive oil."

Salt. "There is no need for active people to restrict all salt, unless they have high blood pressure," says Clark. The average person needs 1,000 to 3,000 milligrams of sodium per day (one teaspoon of salt has about 2,000 milligrams of sodium). During exercise, you do lose some sodium through sweat, but Clark says your body usually adapts to the heat by conserving salt and proportionately sweating more water.

Sodium deprivation is rare since plenty of sodium occurs naturally in foods, and if you do need additional salt, you'll crave it. Be aware that the bulk of sodium in the diet comes from prepared products like canned soups and even cereals and desserts, not from the saltshaker.

Joan is partial to snacking on chips to satisfy her cravings. "I must feel that I need the salt," she says. "I don't shake salt on my food or in my cooking. I know I pick up salt through a variety of different foods, but I eat chips when I crave a concentrated dose of salt. At least I try to choose more nutritional chips, natural or organic, as opposed to those with preservatives."

Alcohol. Beer and other forms of alcohol can be problematic for a runner who drinks before or after exercise. Alcohol of any kind has a dehydrating effect that will get you running—right to the toilet. You'll even feel this drying effect into the next day.

Because of the carbohydrates, some runners think of beer as a sports drink. But alcohol does not replace valuable fluids, nor is it a good source of energy. Nutritionally, alcohol only provides empty calories that are burned preferentially to dietary fat, so you're more likely to add to your body fat stores. So if you're dieting, alcohol is a double-barreled threat.

If you're going to have a postexercise beer, Clark suggests drinking a few glasses of water first and then eating something. Drinking on an empty stomach can heighten the depressant effect of alcohol.

Caffeine. Some runners swear by a preworkout cup of coffee or other caffeinated beverage believing it helps pep them up. Moderate doses of caffeine (the amount in about two cups of coffee) can have an energizing effect. Plus, caffeine stimulates the release of fatty acids, providing a source of energy. Some, however, suffer acid stomach and the jitters. The effects of caffeine depend on personal sensitivity and habit.

If you're used to drinking a cup of coffee before a run or race, by all means do so. Too much caffeine, though, can backfire, particularly before a race, as it adds to the effects of adrenaline. And you're likely to be already pumped up. Caffeine is also a diuretic and leads to frequent trips to the toilet.

Runners Who Shun Meat

Pasta reigns supreme and red meat is out—that's the traditional table talk of many runners, who often see vegetarianism as a healthy choice. Simply avoiding meat does not guarantee a healthy diet. As Clark says, "It's the fat in meat that's the health culprit, not the meat itself."

Many vegetarian diets are low in protein, Clark points out, and consequently low in iron, which is particularly detrimental to women. Protein and iron deficiency can cause fatigue. To get a full complement of essential amino acids (the building blocks of protein), vegetarians should add milk products to meals or combine grains and beans, like beans and rice or chili with corn tortillas. It's not necessary to eat these foods all at the same meal. As long as they're combined within a reasonable time, say, over eight to ten hours, they should form complete proteins in the body.

Athletes who carefully plan a vegetarian diet, using alternate sources of protein, with adequate iron and zinc can meet their nutritional needs. Pure vegans—those who eat no animal products—should take vitamin B_{12} supplements.

Those who are hit-or-miss about protein in their diets, Clark suggests, or experience needless fatigue, might want to consider the benefits of small portions of lean meats such as a thin roast beef sandwich, flank steak stir-fried with broccoli or extra-lean hamburger added to spaghetti sauce.

Joan notes, "I do eat red meat once or twice a week. Some days I feel I really need it. I don't hesitate to make a special trip to the store to get exactly the type I crave."

Eating on the Run

Women runners who are balancing job, exercise and family are among the busiest people. With a full schedule, good eating habits require some careful planning. Co-author Gloria Averbuch and Clark offer their strategies for eating smart despite a busy schedule.

- Keep the basics on hand—powerhouse foods that together give optimum nutrition: low- or nonfat dairy products, dark green vegetables (broccoli and spinach), whole-grain cereals, breads and lean meats such as London broil, boneless chicken breast or ground turkey.
- For freshness and convenience, purchase small amounts of precut fresh vegetables and fruit from salad bars (dig down low to get the coldest, best-kept produce).
- If shopping or meal planning involving perishables seems difficult, consider frozen vegetables. In winter, they may contain more nutrients than fresh, which spend more time in transit from harvest to table.
- Use your freezer. Bread, milk, blanched fresh vegetables, almost

anything can be frozen. Frozen portion sizes ensure freshness and convenience.

• If the thought of preparing meals after a busy day leaves you flat, try a weekend cooking day, during which you and family members prepare and freeze meals for the week.

Busy women exercisers, often very health conscious, have devised some resourceful ways to accommodate good eating while on the go. Gloria got into the carry-along habit during a time of special nutritional needs: exercising during her pregnancies—when timing and food value are especially important. She still continues these habits for herself and her family.

• Have a purse? Pack nonperishables such as crackers and rice cakes, pretzels and dried fruit. Replenish regularly to maintain a permanent supply.

• Pack water or juices (watered down) in small, plastic, reusable water bottles with a screw top.

• Refrigeration isn't always necessary. Yogurt and cheese contain bacteria that prevent spoilage and can be kept at room temperature for a few hours. Don't leave them in a hot car—that's inviting trouble.

• Pack a frozen serving that will thaw out in time for lunch or a snack.

• Add variety to your packed foods. Include cooked vegetables or dinner leftovers. Gloria's daughters' favorite finger food is still baked yams—one of the most nutrient-dense foods. It's best when kept whole, the top peeled and held like an ice cream cone.

If You Run to Lose Weight, Read This

No doubt about it, one of the top reasons many women get into running is to lose weight or to control their weight. Running is easy yet effort-intensive—a continual act of picking up your own body weight step after step. That uses a lot of energy, which comes from burning calories.

Still, women—and this includes athletes as well—seem to struggle harder than men to lose weight. That's because women are meant to carry more fat than men. Whereas 3 to 5 percent of a man's weight is essential fat, women carry 11 to 13 percent essential fat (primarily in the breasts, hips and thighs).

If you eat appropriately and let your appetite be your guide, you will maintain your weight. Even if you overdo it one day, your appetite will adjust your level of hunger the next day. It seems, says Clark, that lean people tend to have a better ability to listen to their appetites than heavier people who can consistently overeat, which is often because of stress and not hunger.

COMPUTING CALORIES

What's the right number of calories for you? The calculation is simple. If you are the average person (and you probably are, believe it or not), follow this rule of thumb.

1. Multiply your weight by 10 to determine your resting metabolic rate—the amount of energy you need simply to exist, regardless of whether you exercise or not. If you weigh 120 pounds, for example, you need about 1,200 calories merely to pump blood, grow hair, breathe and so forth.

2. Add half that number for general daily activities, like working, shopping or brushing teeth. Trim or inflate this amount by 100 calories if you are more sedentary (say, recovering from knee surgery) or more active (like chasing toddlers around all day). In our example, add 600 calories for the 120-pound woman who is moderately active.

3. Add calories for purposeful exercise. The 120-pound woman who trains hard for an hour each day may need an additional 400 calories, bringing her daily total to 2,200 calories per day (1,200 + 600 + 400). Runners burn 85 to 110 calories per mile, depending on body weight (100 to 150 pounds).

Settle on a weight that is comfortable to maintain, even if it's a few pounds above your ideal. As Clark points out, a few added pounds in a fit, active person is likely to be muscle, which can help improve performance.

Dieting: Don't Get Carried Away

What happens when the scale stops tipping in your chosen direction? Clark says there are several factors that can cause your weight to plateau.

First of all, the less you eat, the more your body adapts to eating less. That is, if you hit a plateau, your body may be used to living on fewer calories.

Second, sometimes a plateau is caused by a shift in body fluids as you take on some water weight. The number on the scale may remain the same, or even go up, but you can still be losing fat. You will likely see the scale start to tip down again after this cycle is over.

Third, be reasonable. You may be "programmed" to weigh a certain amount and no less. You may have hit a plateau because you are at or below your genetically determined weight—and your body is saying "no more." Going below your genetic weight usually means you're going too far, and you could be compromising your health.

"Just as there is no 'right height' there is no 'right weight,'" Clark points out. And weight, she says, like height, is largely ruled by your genes. "Seventy percent of weight is genetic. To estimate your natural weight, go to a family reunion and take a good look at your relatives. You'll see a reasonable indication of the weight Mother Nature designed for you, like it or not."

Weight Loss: Just the Facts

When trying to lose weight, it can be quite a struggle to drop even a few pounds. So as you work to shed some unwanted pounds, keep these diet tips in mind.

- Exercise may kill your appetite but not for long. In a couple of hours, you'll likely be hungry again. The temporary loss of appetite is partly because of a rise in body temperature. Exercise in a cold environment, however, like swimming or skiing, makes your temperature drop and thus may make you feel ravenous.

• Spartan daytime eating followed by heavy evening bingeing is a common mistake among dieters. Research shows that you may, in fact, gain weight more easily this way because you are likely to be so hungry by evening that you overeat. Also, you're less likely to burn off those calories as efficiently in the evening as you would earlier in the day. Clark says that "you're going to eat the calories eventually, so why hold off until evening? If you're hungry in the morning, eat." She adds, "If you're not hungry in the morning, chances are you ate your breakfast calories the night before."

• There's no proof that you lose weight faster with low-intensity "fat-burning" exercise (as opposed to high-intensity exercise, which burns more glycogen). To calculate weight loss, you have to look at the whole day's calorie balance and the total energy spent, says Clark, not just the type of fuel burned during exercise.

• "Many dieters believe that snacking is bad," says Clark. "But hunger is neither bad nor wrong. It's normal for a person to get hungry every four hours. If you eat breakfast at 8:00 a.m. and lunch at noon, you can expect to be hungry for a snack at 4:00 p.m. The problem is not snacking but eating the wrong snacks or getting so hungry that you crave sweets or fats and lack the presence of mind needed to make wise food choices."

• Is avoiding dietary fat your best approach to losing weight? Many women runners shun any form of fat in food—believing that fat makes fat. While avoiding excess fat is your best bet for good health and weight control, extreme denial of fat-containing foods may lead to binges.

• Calories count, too. In her counseling, Clark reminds people that weight control is based on a calorie budget as well as a fat budget. Fat loss occurs when you burn off more calories than you eat. According to Clark, the kind of calories may be of lesser consequence. So if you overindulge in carbohydrates, you can still gain weight on a low-fat diet.

• Muscle burns more calories than other tissue. Clark recommends, therefore, that if you want to increase calorie intake without getting fat, build muscle by strength-training exercises, such as weight training or calisthenics.

• You may feel you eat very little, exercise rigorously and still fail to lose weight. If you're gaining weight despite your best efforts, perhaps a nutritionist can help you understand why.

When Running Spurs Out-of-Control Dieting

It's a more common sight every day, especially among adolescents and young women: the woman athlete who works too hard, who regiments her life too much and who often looks—and is—just too thin. To get that way, she may have developed some odd eating habits. In fact, she may have a serious eating disorder.

Until about 20 years ago, few people had even heard of anorexia

THE MYTH OF THE PERFECT RUNNING PHYSIQUE

Too many women hold onto the notion that "thin is in" or that good distance runners have to have a streamlined physique. But that's not necessarily true, says Joan.

"I don't have the stereotypical tall and lean runner's physique. In fact, I sometimes think people look at me and wonder how I've become an elite runner. I'm very small and compact, yet I'll never think of myself as skinny. I've run long enough to know that although I may not be tall and leggy, I get optimal use of my innate efficiency.

"Still, I feel I can relate to the many women runners who feel ambivalent about their bodies and who struggle with their body image. My philosophy is that you have to learn how to love your body and relate to it with respect and gratitude. Although there have been times when I've had my lapses—when I've worried that I or bulimia. Lately, these two eating-behavior disorders are increasingly in the news. One thing needs to be made clear, though: Thinness alone does not point to a nutritional problem.

Anorexia, more properly termed *anorexia nervosa*, is an intense fear of becoming obese and an unrealistic body image. Being five to ten pounds underweight doesn't make you anorexic—weighing less than 85 percent of what you should for your age and height coupled with refusal to gain an ounce more is cause for alarm. The syndrome often includes obsessive dieting, spartan eating habits and exercising for the sheer desire to burn every last calorie consumed. Bulimia is defined as bouts of uncontrolled food bingeing followed by purging through vomiting or use of laxatives (or both).

What's more, anorexia and bulimia are not all-or-nothing disorders. Sports nutrition consultant Jaime S. Rudd, R.D., says you can

should lose a bit of weight—I know that my body has worked for me, and I respect it for what it has delivered. Some of the best runners are not necessarily that thin. Thankfully, the 1990s seem to be a time of shifting away from 'thin for thin's sake' and shifting toward an emphasis on a healthy- and strong-looking body.

"I eat what I want. I can't fuel my workout with a few celery sticks and a bit of dry rice. I want a full meal. Sometimes, my appetite increases and I put on a little extra weight. At these times, I feel that my body is replenishing its stores and rebuilding itself. This normal process is nothing to worry about. If your weight creeps up at other times—when you're tapering for a race, experiencing premenstrual binges or recovering from injury—don't become overly concerned. Do what I do: Tell yourself, I've been here before; this, too, will pass."

have some symptoms of anorexia and bulimia without suffering from the actual disorder.

"Stressful times can bring out a person's desire to binge or restrict food intake," Clark says. "That's why, at holiday times for example, I'm very busy counseling people who are struggling with food."

All this wouldn't necessarily be relevant in a book on running for women, except for one thing: Running is, all too often, one of the calorie burners that anorexic women use to perpetuate their condition.

The effect of a full-blown eating disorder can be devastating. Joan has seen athletes who are driven in many ways. "Compulsive eating is like compulsive training. There's intense training that's compulsive but not self-destructive—such as the kind of training that is part of a reasonable competition goal. If someone is possessed by training, however, I don't believe she'll last long. She will break down at some point from injury, burnout or poor eating habits. She will simply be unable to maintain that unhealthy level of intensity."

Studies have shown that body image—which contributes to eating disorders—isn't related as much to the actual shape and state of the body as to the level of self-esteem. Simply put, self-esteem and self-acceptance are at the heart of a healthy body image.

Special Needs of Women

Across the board, women need more calcium and iron and folic acid than men, and at certain times in life, their needs for other nutrients are increased as well.

Calcium. Calcium builds strong bones, which are needed by everyone including athletes. When calcium intake is low, bones grow thin because of reduced calcium deposits (osteoporosis). When estrogen levels drop, whether because of menopause or intense training and amenorrhea, the risk of osteoporosis rises. (See page 25 for a discussion of how these factors are related in the female athlete triad.)

To combat osteoporosis, adults between the ages of 25 and 50 and children between the ages of 1 and 10 need at least 800 milligrams of calcium a day; for teens, pregnant women, nursing mothers and women over 50, it's 1,200 milligrams a day. That's three to four servings a day of such calcium-rich foods as milk, yogurt and cheeses (low-fat or nonfat for adults, low-fat or regular for children and regular for children less than 2 years old).

Good nondairy sources of calcium include sardines or salmon with the bones, tofu (processed with calcium sulfate), blackstrap molasses, spinach, broccoli and kale. Calcium-fortified orange juice is another option.

Iron. An important element in red blood cells, iron helps to deliver oxygen to all cells of the body. Women need 15 milligrams of iron daily, as compared to 10 milligrams for men. The need increases for menstruating women and those who eat no red meat, which is the best dietary source of iron. Also, all teenagers, who are growing quickly, and marathoners, who may damage red blood cells during repeated pounding of their feet, need more iron. When iron stores are low, fatigue is often the first clue, but more serious problems may develop if the deficiency becomes severe.

To boost iron intake and iron absorption, follow these tips.

• Eat lean cuts of red meat and pork and the dark meat of poultry. The iron in plant sources (prunes, spinach, whole-grain breads) is poorly absorbed, but some iron is better than none.

• Use cast-iron cookware, especially for acidic foods like tomato-based sauces.

• Choose breads and cereals that are iron-fortified or that contain blackstrap molasses.

• Include a source of vitamin C, such as orange juice or tomatoes, with meals that include iron-rich foods. Acidic solutions aid iron absorption.

• Since coffee and tea interfere with iron absorption, do not drink these beverages with meals containing iron if you are anemic.

• If you decide to take an iron supplement, Clark recommends a daily multivitamin and mineral supplement.

Folic acid (folate). According to Clark, one nutrient of particular concern to women contemplating pregnancy is folic acid, a B vitamin

(continued on page 176)

RECIPES TO FORTIFY THE WOMAN RUNNER

YOGURT SHAKE

A great post-run refresher or breakfast drink. Dates and wheat germ boost the iron content, and the banana adds potassium.

  1   cup nonfat yogurt
½–¾ cup calcium-fortified orange juice
 ¼ cup wheat germ
 ½ ripe banana or 2 or 3 dates or 1 teaspoon honey or molasses (or to taste)

Mix the yogurt, orange juice, wheat germ and banana, dates or honey or molasses in a blender.

Makes about 2 cups depending on additions to the mix.

YOGURT TAHINI DRESSING

Tahini is a smooth paste of sesame seeds that is rich in unsaturated fats. Both the yogurt and the tahini pack a high-calcium punch. To add even more calcium, use the dressing on kale or broccoli.

 1 cup plain nonfat yogurt
 2 tablespoons tahini (or to taste)
 1 or 2 garlic cloves, mashed
½ teaspoon cumin
    Hot sauce, like Tabasco (to taste)
    Soy sauce (to taste)

Blend the yogurt, tahini, garlic, cumin, hot sauce and soy sauce until smooth.

Makes about 1 cup.

FORTIFIED, NONFAT BRAN BREAD OR MUFFINS

An old favorite, adapted from a 1943 edition of *The Joy of Cooking!*

2	cups water or water mixed with calcium-fortified orange juice
2	cups chopped dates or a combination of dates, raisins and prunes
½	cup fat-free egg substitute
¼	cup blackstrap molasses
⅓–½	cup brown sugar (less if you use orange juice)
1	teaspoon vanilla
2	cups whole-wheat flour
2	cups bran
2	teaspoons baking powder
1	teaspoon baking soda
1	cup sunflower seeds or nuts (optional)

Boil the water or water and juice and pour over the dates or date mixture and set aside. In a small bowl, mix the egg substitute, molasses, brown sugar and vanilla. In a large bowl, combine the flour, bran, baking powder, baking soda and seeds or nuts. Mix the wet ingredients into the dry ingredients just until blended; do not overmix. Fold the date mixture into the batter. Place the dough in a lightly oiled loaf pan and bake at 350° for 1 hour. Or spoon into lightly oiled muffin tins and bake for 20 minutes.

Makes 1 loaf or about 18 muffins.

Variation: Replace ¼ cup of flour with wheat germ.

involved in fetal brain development. An optimal intake of folic acid at the time of conception can help reduce certain types of birth defects. Clark recommends that women planning a pregnancy eat foods rich in folic acid, such as oranges, spinach, kale and other green vegetables and take a daily supplement of 400 micrograms of folic acid.

Pregnancy. Pregnant women need more calories than nonpregnant women; pregnant women who exercise need even more calories. As a general rule, you'll need at least 500 extra calories per day above what you normally consume, 60 grams of protein per day (as opposed to an average of 46) and 1,200 milligrams of calcium daily. Don't wait until you discover you're pregnant to start eating right. The growing baby-in-the-making will siphon off what you eat plus iron and calcium previously stored.

While pregnant, Joan followed a fairly normal diet, taking care to meet her increased dietary needs. She chose foods with fewer preservatives and more natural ingredients, which were less processed, and included a multivitamin tablet.

Active or not, many women worry that they will gain excessive weight during pregnancy. But Clark stresses that you can be pregnant without being fat. The weight gained during pregnancy can be accounted for by the baby and the baby's needs. Athletic women who are underweight to begin with commonly gain more weight than the 22 to 27 pounds typically recommended during pregnancy; overweight women may gain less.

Nursing. If you are combining nursing and exercise, increase your fluid intake and calories after delivery. Take in an extra 500 calories (more if you're exercising), 1,200 milligrams of calcium and 65 grams of protein in the first six months of nursing (62 grams of protein in the second six months if you continue to nurse).

Because caring for a newborn is an emotionally charged time in your life, often with considerable stress, it can be hard to keep track of your diet and to determine if your desire to eat relates to being hungry or to stress and fatigue. But it's important to make time for optimum nutrition, which is vital to your pregnancy, recovery from the delivery and your exercise program.

Bon Appétit

Moderation and balance, says Clark, are the keys to nutritional success and the enjoyment of food. As Clark helps us to understand, the best diet results from understanding nutrition basics and avoiding fads and misconceptions.

Joan's diet exemplifies these principles of moderation and balance. Clark feels Joan's approach to eating is particularly refreshing. "I see clients all the time who are obsessed with their diets. Joan's lack of obsession with having the perfect diet but rather one that is balanced, helped her to become number one. She sees food as a source of fuel, not as a source of guilt. She gives herself permission to eat."

In fact, Joan says she "eats just about everything and anything," and despite some small variations, her eating-by-instinct diet turns out to match Clark's general recommendations.

If you have special concerns about your diet, seek out a professional nutritionist, preferably one with a background in sports nutrition. Call the American Dietetic Association referral network at 1-800-366-1655 to find your local sports nutritionist who is a registered dietitian.

CHAPTER 13

DRESS FOR RUNNING SUCCESS

Shoes, Bras and Other Basics

Unlike a lot of other sports, running requires very little in the way of equipment. In fact, all you really need is a good pair of shoes. These days, though, you can benefit from gear that enhances comfort, performance and injury prevention. And as a woman, you can take advantage of the very latest in form and function when it comes to everything from footwear to underwear.

Feet First

Let's start at ground level. Getting the right shoes, with a minimum of trial and error, is fundamental. And running shoes have come a long way.

When Joan first started running in the early 1970s, running-shoe technology was in its infancy. "At the time, there were only men's shoes. My foot was so small that even the smallest size was a little big. I wore them anyway because that's what was available. I remember winning a race and receiving a pair of modern, high-tech running shoes as a prize. They felt so comfortable and like they were custom-made. When I ran in them, I felt a new spring in my step."

Basically, running shoes are categorized as either training or racing. Training shoes are heavier and well-cushioned to hold up and give support during steady, hard training efforts. In contrast, racing shoes are lighter and are designed to help you travel quickly with as little weight as possible. Runners' needs vary considerably and are as different as, say, footprints.

Even though she's of slight build, Joan prefers her training shoes on the heavy side. "My sturdier training shoes offer more cushioning and support during the repeated high impact of intense training. What's more, I like the psychological lift I get when I tie on my lighter racing shoes."

The right shoes have played a key role in Joan's success. "I've benefited from periodically having special training shoes made for my expressed requirements." During high-mileage, high-intensity training, these shoes have helped to prevent injury and to protect her while healing from injury.

Racing shoes, Joan finds, are less complicated to fit than training shoes. "My racing shoes, including those I wore in the 1984 Olympics, have been standard issue, the kind that come right out of the box," she reports.

The perfect shoes fit like they're part of your feet. And when they're wrong, your feet will tell you. Even Joan has felt the pain of ill-fitting shoes. "I've worn shoes that were too small and caused terrible blisters."

Advice from the Top

If you want smart advice on shoes, ask someone who really knows them from the inside out. Having worked for Nike since 1980, marketing manager Tom Hartge offers some shoe-buying tips.

His first piece of advice for women runners is to buy women's shoes. "Most running-shoe manufacturers have put a great deal of effort into their women's lines. At Nike, we have found that women runners' needs in shoes are quite similar to men's. This is because, biomechanically, men and women are more alike than different. Maybe individual runners are more vulnerable to injury, but, as a group, women are not more injury-prone than men."

The big difference is in the last, which is the shape of the shoe sole. Because women, in general, tend to have a narrower heel and midfoot, many women's shoes are designed to reflect this. "But the guts of the men's and women's shoes are the same," claims Hartge.

Of course, several manufacturers make models that fit a variety of foot shapes. Some companies even have women's models for very wide feet.

Although Joan exclusively wore men's shoes up until the 1984 Olympics, she has since switched to women's. But some women still prefer to train in men's shoes—often because they have longer or wider feet or they are attached to a particular model.

Racing shoes, however, are a different case. Most are unisex models. So when shopping for a racing shoe, look for a model that fits your size and width.

Where to Buy

Where you buy shoes can be nearly as important as what you buy. Another important rule from Hartge is to head for a running store to buy your shoes rather than general sports or department stores. "There are at least 100 great running stores across the country. They know the shoes and the sport. Staff members are usually runners, and the selection is usually broader and more varied."

A running-shoe store is also more than just a place to buy. Hartge calls them community centers for runners. "Running-shoe stores are great for shoptalk. You can get informal advice, inquire about training partners or running groups and check out the local races, track sessions and available medical care."

"As an innocent bystander," Joan says, "I've gone into both department stores and running-shoe stores and watched people buy running shoes. It's the difference between night and day. Even from buying my dress shoes I have learned that in the shoe market, service is still worth a lot."

In fact, Joan believes in smart shoe shopping in all categories. As mentioned in chapter 9, her blisters or footaches aren't usually from running shoes. They're from dress shoes, new or ill-fitting ones, or walking longer in them than she expected. "Smart shopping for non-running shoes is just as important as finding good running shoes," she points out.

"I think women are discerning shoppers," believes Hartge, who has also sold shoes in stores. "But men and women alike can be a little intimidated by a running store if they aren't training seriously or haven't run a road race. I think it's even more important for recreational runners—men or women—to go to the right store, where they can be steered away from improper products."

A GOOD FIT

Here are key areas to check when fitting a shoe to your foot. Look for the shoe that:

- Is shaped like your foot.
- Is snug in the heel.
- Has a high toe box—room for your toes to wiggle.
- Has about a finger's width of space in front of your longest toe when you are standing in the shoe.
- Has a good arch support. This support comes from both the midsole and the removable arch support. You should feel the height of the bump hit slightly toward the rear portion of your arch. This protects the heel.
- Has a proper heel counter to provide support at the back of the shoe.
- Has a firm sole. Good rear sole material is an indicator of overall build. The more dense the sole, the more stable the shoe.

Finding Your Shoe Type

Once inside the store, you encounter a wall of shoes with models of every shape and color on display. They're grouped by categories such as walking or cross-training. The running shoes are usually classified as lightweight, cushioning and stability or motion control.

The first category is for racing shoes and lighter training models for runners who are fairly efficient and lightweight and who can get away with wearing a minimal shoe. These softer shoes have a less dense midsole.

Cushioning shoes offer more protection but are designed for runners who have none of the biomechanical problems described in chapter 9. Don't assume that all cushioning shoes are soft. They may feel either soft or firm, if they contain polyurethane.

Fewer people need stability in a shoe, says Hartge, but those who

ORTHOTICS: WORTH CONSIDERING

More and more runners rely on orthotics to modify their footwear. These lightweight inserts fit inside the shoe, replacing the removable insole. Designed by podiatrists, they can change the gait, stress of impact or compensate for a leg-length discrepancy. Orthotics can stabilize foot placement and thereby reduce rotation of the foot while running.

Joan has used orthotics but has had more success with simpler devices—over-the-counter insoles or heel lifts that compensate for her shorter leg. She notes, "In my situation, I don't think orthotics helped. I felt they altered my stride and I wasn't running as efficiently."

It's best to consult a podiatrist or sports medicine specialist if you think orthotics may relieve a running problem.

do are highly dependent on it. This shoe is built to last as long as possible on the medial side (inside) and has a firm midsole that won't let your foot wobble or rotate. These shoes help compensate for such common biomechanical problems as excessive pronation, which is rolling of the feet inward on impact. It is the heaviest shoe type, has a wide base of support and can best accommodate orthotics, which are corrective devices placed inside the shoes.

If you're new to running, expect a trial-and-error period in which you may switch types of shoes. "Most runners don't know what they need until they've been running for a while," Tom Hartge, marketing manager at Nike, points out. If you don't know where to start, ask for a cushioning shoe, which is the middle category in terms of weight and support.

"Don't judge a shoe by its price tag," says Hartge. "Finding the right shoe is the first priority. After determining your needs, a shoe dealer may show you several shoes covering a wide price range." A more expensive shoe usually has more complicated technology and more features. So these shoes may be heavier. But if a woman is smaller and lighter, she may not need that much shoe. "Don't automatically head for a high-tech shoe," says Hartge. "I think you should only wear as much shoe as you need for your body to work as efficiently as it can."

Narrowing Your Choice

Tell the salesperson where you run, how often, how far and what your goals are. If you intend to run a consistent amount of mileage on one type of surface, then one type of shoe may do. If you change surfaces, want to try speed work or more miles or a race—you may benefit from two separate pairs. For any change in training, you might want to head back to the store to inquire about new shoes.

Racing shoes and training shoes are not interchangeable, except for a small number of thin, elite runners. You should buy a racing shoe only if you're serious about competition or want to feel faster and can go lighter without getting hurt. These shoes are designed to benefit those who are quick enough to run up on their toes, as they're geared to propel off the forefoot.

Racing shoes carry the risk of less support. The heel surface width is 35 percent less narrower than that of training shoes. On the other hand, if you have no problem with injuries, wearing special shoes for speed work or competition may give you a psychological edge.

Take your current running shoes into the shoe store when looking for a new pair. "Every shoe tells a story," says Hartge, "and a good shoe salesperson can read that story." Pick up your current shoes and look at the bottoms. It's an imprint of your running style. The wear pattern on the sole tells you the type of runner you are. For example, the amount of wear on the bottom outer soles (not the inner area, as many believe) indicates to what degree your feet pronate. The wrinkles visible in the midsole show compression.

As most experienced runners know, Joan tells people, when you've found a shoe you like, stay with it. This can be difficult when your shoe company changes models. "Manufacturers are always trying to improve their shoes while not alienating fans of an existing model. The object of a new model is to add better features while keeping the strengths of the current shoe," says Hartge.

When you're trying on shoes, simulate running conditions as closely as possible. Wear the socks you run with and shop in the late afternoon when your feet are usually the most expanded. Don't just stand on the carpet in the store. Most good stores have either a hard surface, treadmills or a track to test shoes. Some stores even let you run outside on the street.

How do you ultimately judge if the shoe is right for you? Joan's bottom-line prescription is a good one: "They should feel great from the beginning. Sometimes you can try on shoes and your legs just don't respond. It's like they're in cement casts. There's no spring. You feel as if the shoes just stick to the ground. I can tell right away when this happens."

Beware of the sense that you need to break them in. The right shoe gives a secure fit and makes you feel like you do on your best running day—peppy, bouncy and swift of foot. You'll get the "feeling" even with a short jog in the store.

What about the size? Don't get upset if you need a larger shoe size.

Running shoes often run bigger than street shoes; your size 7 loafer may translate to a 7½ or even an 8 running shoe. The main consideration is proper fit and comfort.

If you're in doubt, wear the shoes around the house for up to a week. You can take them back if you decide they aren't right. Most stores have a flexible return policy.

How long should a running shoe last? Experts often define shoe life in number of miles run. But Hartge doesn't like to do that. "A shoe may feel worn out, despite the fact that you're supposed to get another 100 miles out of it. Don't hold your shoes to miles. Go on a gut feeling. If the shoe feels flat, there's no zip and your legs are dead, it's time for another pair." Another good way to tell if it's time to retire old shoes is to try on an old shoe with a new one. If the contrast is stark, get a new pair.

How Many Pairs?

Some runners believe that using more than one pair of shoes prolongs shoe life. Joan uses two pairs and introduces a third before retiring the oldest set at around 300 miles. She believes that with a different pair of shoes the wear—specifically the stress—changes between runs and that this helps her avoid injury. Hartge says, however, that "if you do the mathematics, trading off probably doesn't prolong the actual running life of the shoe. But it feels like it does. If you have the money and you like a change, buy a couple of pairs."

Handle with Care

Take good care of your running shoes, and you'll get the maximum mileage from them. As a rule, do not put shoes in the washing machine. If it's necessary, an occasional trip through in cold water on a gentle cycle is okay. You can clean mud or dirt by dousing the shoes with a hose or by using a toothbrush and soap. Prop the shoes up against a wall; it helps them dry better. To avoid smelly shoes, pull out the insoles—which absorb sweat—to dry after running. Also, says Joan, another way to avoid smelly shoes is always to run with socks. Extreme heat is not good for shoes—this includes running them in the clothes dryer and leaving them in intense sun or in a heated car.

Resoling shoes was once popular, but it's not a good idea. Once the outer sole is worn, the midsole is usually shot, which means less support on impact. "Shoes are like automobile tires," says Joan. "Just like it isn't safe to drive with worn tires, worn running shoes will probably lead to problems."

A Strong Foundation: Choosing a Bra

It was right after she finished her first marathon—extensively bloodied by a bra that chafed—that LaJean Lawson decided to get into bra research, which she did for both a masters and a doctorate degree. An adjunct professor in exercise science at Oregon State University in Corvallis, she is also a consultant to seven companies that manufacture bras.

This is one area in which all women are not created equal, Dr. Lawson emphasizes. "Because running is one of the highest-impact sports on the breasts, you need a lot of motion control. Research is teaching us how much more of that control we need for C, D and DD sizes."

That's why proper bras are essential and more problematic for the larger-breasted women. Does this mean, then, that smaller-breasted women can go without a bra like Joan does? "From a support point of view, it may be true that a woman can run braless, but a bra can help protect tender skin and draw off sweat," says Dr. Lawson. Abrasion and infections can develop when shirt fabric rubs against the skin. Women who choose to run braless, however, can help avoid that problem by putting adhesive bandages over their nipples.

Most of the time Joan chooses to run without a bra. "I'm not very big and I feel more constricted with a bra," she explains. "Also, I used to worry about slipping straps. Now they make singlets with strap holders." Joan laughs as she suggests, "Perhaps they created those holders as a result of my running in the Olympics with my bra strap hanging out!"

What to look for. There are three types of sports bras: compression, those that separate the breasts and a few models that do both. Another form of support is called the Airborn, which is a bralike halter top for smaller-breasted women that is made for various sports and exercise. Compression bras are generally best for smaller-breasted women, Dr. Lawson says, because these bras have a lot of elastic materials in them. The weight of large breasts quickly breaks down elastic, however. Also, larger-breasted women often are worse off with these bras, as they create a rubber band effect, resulting in excessive bouncing.

A good sports bra should have straps that don't slip and seams that feel smooth. Try out bras by moving, stretching, running in place and wiggling around. Check for potential problems from all seams by actually rubbing them against an area of sensitive skin, such as the armpits. A bra should be snug, but you should be able to take a deep breath comfortably.

Larger-breasted women often get best support from separate, molded cups. Check these bras for minimal stretch by grabbing the straps and the bottom of the bra and pulling. It shouldn't stretch much. When you try it on, there should be just enough stretch to allow you to raise your arms and that stretch should come in the back of the bra when you put your arms down.

"Bras are like shoes," says Dr. Lawson, "they can protect you, but they have their limits." Even the best bras will take a beating over the long run. Apply petroleum jelly or a similar gel under any potential chafing areas. It also helps to change bras from run to run and to discard old bras promptly.

Where to buy. Because it can be intimidating for some women to seek sales help when buying bras, Dr. Lawson recommends heading for a women's sports specialty store, if possible. A female clerk in a department store can advise on fit, she says, but may not know whether the product is right for your sport. A running store may offer a good choice if you don't feel self-conscious at the possibility of buying from a young, male clerk.

How to care for bras. As for any garment, bra care is important. A good sports bra is made of the same performance materials as other running clothing. Despite what a care label says, Dr. Lawson feels that it's smart to forgo the dryer for a clothesline. "Both heat and bleach can weaken the material," she warns.

Good Gear Keeps You Going

Running wear has gone high-tech with colorful tights that fit like a second skin, featherweight jackets, Velcro pockets and tabs. Bright and beautiful running clothes can give you a psychological lift, but they do more than make you look good. They ensure that you can run comfortably year-round in heat, cold, rain, wind, snow—or any combination.

Clothing doesn't just protect you from the elements; it can actually improve the quality of your running. That's why running gear is referred to in the industry as performance products, says Mary Ellen Smith, director of materials research for Nike Apparel. Smith also points out that the running clothes on the market have been adapted from those used in competition. If, for example, you wear tights—something close to your legs—they keep you the least encumbered, which helps you to move faster. But on your torso, it's not beneficial to wear something skintight. The material needs to breathe, wicking away perspiration and releasing body heat as you run.

Although outfitting yourself in state-of-the-art gear costs more than a standard-issue gray sweat suit, Smith believes that much of the modern gear is worth considering. "Think of it as investing in essential equipment. That's the perspective that a serious runner needs to take.

SEE AND BE SEEN

You need to be seen when running in the morning or evening darkness. Some running gear comes with reflective areas, or you can apply reflective strips. Running companies market "lite," or night fluorescent, clothing, but the treated portions do wear off eventually with washing.

The best investment is a special reflective vest that covers your chest and back. You can also buy the same material in reflective belts, headbands and leg and armbands. The vest is a lot more visible than the relatively small portions of reflective material on shoes or jackets.

I've found that once people get into performance products, they all say the same thing: 'I never knew how comfortable I could feel!'"

As comfort is the main objective, clothing materials need to be not only breathable but soft. For both, look for microfibers, like Coolmax and polypropylene. "It feels almost buttery to the touch," says Smith. This clothing serves many purposes. First, it is comfortable next to the skin. Second, it does a good job moving moisture away from the skin. It is also such a versatile material that it can be part of a range of running gear. For example, microfibers can be woven so tightly that the material will be rain-resistant.

Here are some tips on seasonal dressing.

How Hot Is It?

When the temperature climbs, you want to be cool. One material that works well is mesh, which lets sweat evaporate quickly. This is the minimalist approach.

The next level is a synthetic/cotton blend that will absorb any excess moisture that doesn't evaporate. For hot or humid conditions, the material used by most manufacturers is Coolmax. Polyester next to the skin is preferred over something nonabsorbent, like nylon, which tends to get wet and stick to the body.

Of course, the cotton T-shirt is a classic, and a standard for Joan. While T-shirts may get clammy and heavy for sweatier runners, Joan prefers them. She sweats lightly and likes both the extra sun protection and the feel of cotton next to her skin. In fact, all her gear—a mixture of both traditional and high-performance products—reflects her belief in finding what works and staying with it.

For woven fabrics for shorts, a texture next to the skin like supplex or woven polyester doesn't absorb moisture so it won't stick to the body like nylon does.

When It's Freezing Outside

How do you dress to stay warm without turning into a human sauna once your exercise generates some heat? The goal of winter wear is to keep you warm enough and to wick the perspiration from the skin so you don't get a chill or a clammy feeling. On top of that, you need protection from rain and wind. Joan, who has to dress for the notoriously cold Maine winters, combines the new with the tried-and-true. While she may wear a cotton turtleneck under her microfiber windbreaker, she wears Lycra tights on her legs.

Rule number one, according to Smith, is to never wear absorbent material next to the skin. That means no cotton, silk or wool. Choose synthetics like polyester or polypropylene to wick perspiration away from the body. Every company has some brand of this type of clothing, says Smith. Microfiber, or treated polyester tights—made in various thicknesses—helps move moisture. Some runners wear them underneath running shorts or underwear. Smith suggests buying underwear made from synthetic fibers. If you prefer to run in something less clingy than Lycra tights, looser pants, which are heavier in weight, are available in a 50/50 cotton/polyester blend. Lightweight wind-protection pants—made of nylon taffeta—can also be worn over tights.

In general, the smartest strategy for winter wear is layering, particularly on top. The first layer next to the skin should be the moisture-transportation layer. Turtlenecks or crewnecks made from Thermax are popular. On a really cold day, some runners wear a second layer.

The final, or outer, layer provides protection from the elements. But even this top layer should be breathable. It should keep heat in and allow the moisture from perspiration out. "It's been hard for people to shake the idea they were sold in the 1980s that you must have waterproof material," says Smith. "What you need is water-resistant and breathable fabrics." The materials promoted in the 1980s were laminates, like Gortex. That's better for less-aerobic activity, says Smith. Running jackets come with a nylon outer lining and a mesh inner lining for light weight. These are good insulators and best for fall-like weather. For colder weather, sturdier jackets feature a wind-proof, water-resistant outer layer and an insulated inner layer.

Covering the Extremities

No matter how warm your torso, if your head, hands or feet are chilly, you'll be miserable. Here's what to do to cope with the effects of weather.

Gloves. Hands, like all extremities, need extra protection. Runners choose anything from gloves to mittens or socks—or layers combining them. Joan often wears two pairs at once. Experiment to see what's best for you. Thermax gloves are state of the art—warm but lightweight and breathable.

Hats. In warm weather, a hat protects both your head and face from the sun. For this purpose, a visor or a lightweight cap is a good choice. Many runners prefer visors because they allow heat to be diffused by not covering the head, while they protect the face. Joan's signature racing hat is her baseball or painter's cap. The baseball cap was with her when she won her first Boston Marathon in 1979, and the painter's cap was on her head when she won the 1984 Olympic Marathon.

In winter, covering one's head becomes essential, as most of the body's heat is lost through the top of the head. A wool hat is fine for the short run but for longer sessions, use polyester fleece. It's lighter

BE AN INFORMED CONSUMER

To be a smart shopper, a bit of technical information can go a long way. "I have a lot of faith in the consumer," states Mary Ellen Smith, director of materials research for Nike Apparel. To help you get in the know, listed below are the names to look for on clothing labels. Better yet, strut your stuff by walking in and asking for these fabrics by name.

- Layer 1. Moisture transportation layer—100 percent polyester knits, treated and untreated, are Coolmax, Thermax, Capilene and Dri-F.I.T.

- Layer 2. Thermal/insulation layer—fleece materials include Therma-F.I.T. and Polar Tec.

- Layer 3. Outer layer—water-resistant breathables include Silmond, Versa-Tech, Clima-F.I.T. and Clima-Guard.

in weight and wicks away perspiration. Wide headbands that cover the ears are also preferred by runners who perspire a lot. On especially cold days, you can combine a headband with a hat. In Maine, Joan wears a fleecelike hat that covers her ears.

Socks. In summer or winter, your feet are sure to sweat, so synthetic fibers, like acrylic or Coolmax, are your best bet. If you have really cold feet, you may want heavier socks. Just make sure the socks are shaped like the foot and fit fairly snug. Tube socks are too thick and may slide into shoes and cause blisters. Special running socks are also marketed as blisterproof, or you can try wearing more than one pair of socks for blister protection.

CHAPTER 14

RUNNING WITH YOUR MIND

Setting Goals, Staying Motivated

Before the 1984 Olympic Marathon, Joan told Bob Sevene, her adviser at the time, "Whoever wants this race the most is going to win it." As she spoke, she realized that she was that person. "At that moment, I just knew I could do it."

The power of the mind in sports cannot be stressed enough. You can train hard, wear the right shoes, follow a healthy diet and peak at the right time, but you also need to establish the right mind-set. As Tom Fleming, an elite athlete, coach and owner of a specialty running store in Bloomfield, New Jersey, tells his athletes, "Success is 90 percent physical and 10 percent mental. But never underestimate the power of that 10 percent."

Feeling Good about Running

Why does running make you feel good? To begin with, it reduces tension and anxiety, has been known to ease depression and builds confidence. It also allows you to leave the rest of the world behind, set aside any worries or negative thoughts and focus on the simple pleasure of the act of running. And it offers a natural high.

Endorphins are the "feel good" brain chemicals triggered by exercise. They've been called natural painkillers and have a calming effect on the nerves and muscles. Endorphins can kick in from the very first run, but they do so at different levels. As you become more conditioned, your body releases more endorphins when you exercise. You may also get the endorphin rush after running, as its effect lasts up to four hours.

For the more experienced runner, endorphins can start to work at any point in the run. The strongest effects of this calming brain chemical, says Linda Bunker, Ph.D., sports psychologist at the University of Virginia in Charlottesville, come with at least 20 minutes of exercise at 80 percent of the maximum heart rate—which is also the formula for a pace quick enough to result in optimal physical fitness.

WHAT MAKES JOAN RUN

To keep running long and hard, day in and day out, Joan uses her head and heart as well as her legs. As you look over some of Joan's motivations, think about your own.

- The social aspect: running with friends or in groups.

- Testing yourself: competition against herself or against others; the discipline of a hard workout.

- A successful friend: seeing or hearing about someone else who does well.

- Good weather: a chance to savor the day—particularly an extraordinarily beautiful day, or a beautiful place.

A Reason to Run: Motivation

Nothing can move your legs down the road if your head and heart don't want to be running. Amby Burfoot, executive editor of *Runner's World* magazine and former Boston Marathon winner, has said that after analyzing all the aspects of training and preparation, only one element is important to him, and that's motivation.

Your reason to run, whether it's a means to an end—like fitness or weight control—or the end itself, can be anything or many things. You may be inspired by a great runner who wins a marathon or the neighbor across the street, whose 10-K time is three minutes faster than yours. The power of the mind drives the body to new levels of performance when you find a way to stay inspired day after day.

"Certain things particularly motivate me in training," says Joan, "like running for time—even beyond its conventional meaning. Being late or not having enough time may seem like a disadvantage, but I use it to motivate myself. So if I leave for a run 15 minutes late (which is not uncommon), rather than shorten my loop, I try to run it faster.

"I use other situations for motivation, too. During my coaching days at Boston University, I ran near the Charles River. I would try to

• A good read: an exceptional or inspiring running article, book or video.

• Wanting to make up for lost time: for missing a run because of bad weather or injury.

• Overcoming adversity: particularly to beat the odds.

• Running for someone else: particularly someone you admire or who has inspired you, such as your coach, a friend or your family.

• The desire to prove yourself and your abilities.

keep pace with the rowers on the river. Keeping my eye on the smooth movement of the shell cutting through the water helped me feel fluid and fast.

"I am also motivated by being watched. An old woman named Amy, who used to sit at her window, would often watch me run by. I always tried to put forth extra effort when I passed her house. I knew she would tell me, as other neighbors have, when I looked tired or sluggish."

A change of scene can also add a spark to your training. Running in a beautiful place that's different from your usual route can spur you on. Even if you have to drive to reach such a site, the inspiration can be worth it. Adds Joan, "I also tend to run unfamiliar courses at a slightly faster pace because I'm always interested in seeing what's around the next bend."

Goals: Stepping Stones to Success

Keep your eye on the prize. By consciously setting goals for yourself, you bolster your motivation. "Goal setting is not a mind game," says Joan. "It is a process of developing the internal willpower to accomplish what you have set out to do."

For Joan, goals range from immediate to very long range. Short-range goals may be those you set for the next week or month, like exercising five days a week; while long-range goals usually extend for six months to a year, like finishing your first marathon. Then there are very long range goals—sometimes called dreams. Joan says, "For so many years, my dream was to win an Olympic gold medal; now, it's to break 2:20 in the marathon or at least be running competitively when that happens."

"Use goals not as ends in themselves but as stepping stones," says Dr. Bunker. "When you reach 80 percent of your long-range goal, reset it." Above all, goals should help motivate and challenge you. "Goals are tools that should work for you," says Dr. Bunker.

"When I talk about goals to groups," Joan says, "I emphasize making them attainable. If obstacles or difficulties appear, set some intermediate goals that you can hit in a shorter amount of time without losing sight of the long-term goal."

You can make goals concrete with tangible symbols. Dr. Bunker suggests writing your goal down on an index card. "Then put it where you will see it, such as in your gym locker or taped to your computer. This reinforces your commitment." Some goals may become so ingrained that they are always in your thoughts. "If it's that important," says Joan, "I don't have to write it down."

Being Confident

Goals are like a staircase. Achieving each one gets you closer to the top and builds your confidence along the way. "We all need to feel competent," says Dr. Bunker. "In psychology, competence equals confidence."

"Good workouts give you confidence and a 'feel good' mood," says Joan. "This mood, in turn, gives added confidence." When it's time to prove your ability in a race, belief in yourself can be the difference.

One of Joan's greatest races was billed as the match of the decade. In the 1985 Chicago Marathon, the three top women marathoners in the world went head-to-head—Joan, Norway's Ingrid Kristiansen and Portugal's Rosa Mota. Joan matched strides with Kristiansen for 17 miles before pulling away to win and setting a new American record of 2:21:21 that, as of this writing, still stands.

"Hang with her," Joan told herself. "This is an awesome pace. One of us is going to break, and it's not going to be me." Joan admits it was a "huge mental relief" when she was finally in the lead. She advises, when you're up against a competitor, "Trust yourself. Tell yourself, as I did, that you find it hard to believe that anyone can be as strong as you, based on your training."

Competition: Many Ways to Win

Competition is a tremendous motivator. "For every runner in a race, there's a goal," says Joan. "Some women want to beat the competition, and some want no part of that. They just want to feel good about themselves and their effort." Running gives you a chance to do both.

Even for the best, successful competition doesn't always mean coming in first. "I can place second, third or fourth," Joan says, "but if I have achieved my goal, I consider myself a winner. I strive to run my best race. Sometimes I'm faster than everyone else, sometimes I'm not, yet I might have set a personal record. I'm satisfied knowing that I ran the best race I was capable of running that particular day."

"Wanting to be better is unique to human beings," says Dr. Bunker. As a runner, you have a choice of options. You can set a chal-

THE MIND/BODY CONNECTION: RELAXATION

The world watched Joan take an early lead and literally run away with an Olympic gold medal. She made it look so easy. "On that day, it was easy," claims Joan. "I'd done the proper homework, was relaxed and ready, and everything seemed to fall into place."

The ease in any great effort stems from relaxation—both mental and physical. Achieving that relaxation is tricky. In the midst of a difficult effort, we may not be aware of the tension of the moment.

Physical relaxation. The night before a big race, Joan practices a bedtime relaxation ritual in which she concentrates on relaxing her entire body from head to toe. It's her way of taking "inventory." She does the same on the morning of the race.

You need not restrict this preparation just to racing. This same process is useful before any training run—from a jog to a speed session. At home or even at the office, take a few moments to close your eyes, breathe and relax before you focus on what you're about to do.

Joan takes cues from other runners as well. "Often, I'll see another runner shake out her arms, and I'll do the same. Sure enough, it loosens me up, too," she says.

Play the "1 to 5 Game." When you run, you are not intensely working your entire body, but you're not being a rag doll, either. Your upper body needs to be very loose but not your legs and feet. To practice finding a balance in relaxing different body parts,

lenge with objective measures like time or distance, or you can compete against someone else. You may begin with the first type of competition and progress to the second or use a combination of the two. But don't automatically shy away from wanting to beat someone else.

play the "1 to 5 Game" developed by Linda Bunker, Ph.D., sports psychologist at the University of Virginia in Charlottesville, for the runners she works with.

A lot of tension—like making a tight fist—is a 5; ultimate relaxation—like a drooping head—is a 1. What you're looking for in your running, says Dr. Bunker, is a 3 in your upper body and a 5 in your lower body. During a practice session, Dr. Bunker gives various commands, such as "Make your face a 5 and your arm a 1." This allows the athlete to isolate the tightening/relaxation effort and thus become more conscious of it.

Mental relaxation. "I think you can relax your mind much the same way you do your body," says Joan. "To stay relaxed, keep an open, positive mind. Don't let negativity or doubt enter—like unfavorably comparing yourself to other runners. In fact, it's always best, especially before a race, to surround yourself with supportive people."

Get rid of those negative thoughts. Dr. Bunker asks her runners to express any negative thoughts to their teammates while running. Partners often tell each other, "I can't make it; I'm hurting; I'm too slow." Nothing switches that thought faster than a response like, "We're on a record pace" or "It's only 200 yards more." Try it. Talking to a running partner about your negative feelings can often get them out of the way.

On the other hand, don't let yourself be subtly coerced into pushing too hard. Cautions Dr. Bunker, "Be careful not to be forced into it by someone else. Decide what's best for you."

A pivotal period in Joan's career was the year at North Carolina State where she battled to keep up in training with top running sisters Julie and Mary Shea. "While on one level I learned through this experience to tolerate a higher level of pain, I also never recovered enough for my races." On the whole, because she was out of her environment and her own running rhythm, it was not a happy year for Joan.

Positive Mind Power

As you train your body to race, you train your mind. The last 48 hours before a race, for example, should be reserved for positive thinking only. "During that time, champions visualize themselves running the best race of their lives. They see themselves crossing the finish line victoriously," says Dr. Bunker.

In Joan's case, "I think of races I've won or done well in. I replay positive images of training runs where I've felt myself floating." Of her Olympic victory she says, "I concentrated on what I was doing and what I wanted, not on the credentials of the other women. I felt in control, even though I knew the runners behind me thought I was crazy for taking the lead so early." Her motto is "The person who feels in control is going to control the race."

In contrast, the 1993 Boston Marathon in the hot, muggy weather shook her confidence. Joan questioned her ability in the heat and altered her goals, something she says is never good to do before a race. In the end, she finished in sixth place. "If you're very focused and motivated, things like a bad meal, the weather, your period—all of that shouldn't affect you," she says.

For Joan, feeling nervous is a necessary part of racing well. You can view it by saying to yourself, "I'm so nervous I can't race," or, like most good athletes—including Joan—you can say, "This means I'm really ready." In fact, many top runners have said that when the pre-race nervousness disappears, it's time to hang up the shoes and retire from competition.

"Wanting to be better is why we continue to train and to compete," says Joan. "I have sacrificed a lot—willingly—and worked very hard. I still want to do my best and improve. That is why twice a year, at the most, I can muster enough focus to prepare for a marathon. Part of that focus includes an optimistic outlook. Whether you're facing a major race or the prospect of summoning energy for a daily run, my advice is to work to make it as positive an experience as you can."

So don't bring negativity out on a run. To help you leave your troubles behind, Dr. Bunker has some suggestions. When you tie on your running shoes, imagine your emotional "baggage" being left behind with your other shoes. Or consider that closing the door as you head out is a literal as well as figurative act. Dr. Bunker points out, "You don't carry your groceries when you run, why should you carry your mental baggage with you? It'll still be there when you stop running."

If negative thoughts come to mind during your run, imagine changing the channel as you do on your television. "You're in control of the channels," says Dr. Bunker. "Click off a bad thought."

Remember endorphins? Well, Dr. Bunker says that you can actually negate the effect of these positive brain chemicals by creating and caving in to feelings of stress. Help the endorphins flow by keeping your thinking positive. Let your running be unimpeded by negativity, or, as Bunker puts it, "Get out of the way of your run."

Be a Dreamer

As a child, Joan's dream was to go to the Olympics. Dreams like that can be lofty; they're supposed to be. Joan's dreams may be different from yours, but, as Dr. Bunker says, a dreamer is a winner, whatever she dreams.

Again, it goes back to having a positive outlook. "Winners say what they want to happen. Losers say what they feel will happen," says Dr. Bunker. The best runners, she says, like Joan, are characterized by their confidence and optimism. They are not doubters; they are believers. They are also dreamers.

Joan is a typical dreamer—in the true sense of the word. So adamant was she to realize her dream that she was able to overcome tremendous adversity and was willing to take big risks. Points out Dr.

Bunker, "Who's to say how fast anyone can recover from knee surgery? Joan may be in that 1 percent who can do it in 17 days. And who's to say if her pace in the beginning of a marathon is too fast? We often see what were believed to be impossible feats in all athletes who make breakthroughs," she concludes.

"I guess I am a dreamer," confirms Joan. "I know what I think I'm capable of. Even though I had knee surgery before the Olympic trials, I had so much faith in my training and in my dream and that kept me going—even though the odds were against me."

So why not be a runner like Joan Samuelson? Remember, she took the lead in the Olympic Games and never looked back. As Dr. Bunker concludes from Joan's feat, "Why not be a dreamer instead of being a follower?"

ABOUT THE AUTHORS

Joan Benoit Samuelson won a gold medal in the first women's Olympic Marathon in Los Angeles in 1984. She has bettered the American record in the marathon four times—still the four fastest times ever run by an American woman—and currently holds the women's American marathon record of 2:21:21, set in Chicago in 1985. The former world-record holder in the marathon, Samuelson also holds scores of other records and has a long list of victories in some of the most prestigious road races, such as the Falmouth Road Race.

Samuelson was a three-time all-American cross-country and track-and-field athlete while in college and has been designated Runner of the Year at least four times by *Runner's World, Running Times* and *Track & Field News*. Her honors include the Jesse Owens Award, Sullivan Award, Bowdoin Prize, Tufts Jumbo Award and Kiputh Award from Yale University.

Samuelson is a consultant to Nike and travels regularly as a motivational speaker. She participates in numerous running clinics across the country and has coached women's cross-country and long-distance running at Boston University.

In 1986, a statue of Joan was erected in her hometown of Cape Elizabeth, Maine.

Joan Samuelson lives in Freeport, Maine, with her husband, Scott, and their two children, Abigail and Anders.

Gloria Averbuch is a running and fitness writer and the author of four books, including the *New York Road Runners Club Complete Book of Running* with Fred Lebow. Her articles have appeared in such publications as *Vogue,* the *New York Times, Ms.* and *Runner's World*. A daily runner who competes in road races as well, she is a features editor for *New York Running News* and a consultant for the New York Road Runners Club, where she has been employed since 1979. Her radio broadcasts on running and fitness can be heard on WABC and WFAN in New York City.

Averbuch lives in Upper Montclair, New Jersey, with her husband, Paul Friedman, and their two daughters, Yael and Shira.

INDEX

Note: <u>Underscored</u> page references indicate boxed text. **Boldface** references indicate illustrations.

A

Acclimatization, 67, 68
Achilles tendinitis, 116–17, 118, 143
Achilles tendons
  inflammation of, 116–17, 118, 143
  massaging, 140
  pain in, 116–17, 129
  stretching, 118, 136, **136**
Acid stomach, 164
Active isolated (AI) stretching, 132
Adolescents
  puberty's effects on running and, 45
  training and, 43–44
Adrenaline, 22, 93, 164
Advanced runners
  marathon training for, 78, <u>88–89</u>
  10-K training for, 75–76
Advil, 17. *See also* Ibuprofen
Advil Mini-Marathon, 103, <u>109</u>
Age groups
  adolescents
    puberty's effects on running and, 45
    training and, 43–44
  children
    competition and, 44
    love of running and, 41–42
    mentoring, 44–45
    nutrition and, 45–46
    parents and, 42–43, 45

puberty and, 45
  role models for, 42–43
  masters, 47–48
  over-fifty, 47
  over-forty, 46–50
  pre-teens, 43–44
Aging, muscles and, 48, 129
Airborn bras, 186–87
AI stretching, 132
Alaska Run for Women 8-K, <u>109</u>
Alcohol, poor nutrition and, 163–64
Amenorrhea, 23–26, 30, 46
American College of Sports Medicine, 25
American Dietetic Association, 177
Anabolic steroids, 28
Anaprox, 18
Anderson, Bob, 130
Anderson, Owen, 9
Anorexia, 170–72
Anti-inflammatory medications, 17, 18, 20, 121, 124, 125
Antioxidants, good nutrition and, 162
Antiseptics, 115–16
Appetite, 166–67, 168
Arch, foot, 117–18
Arms, swinging while running, 126
Arthroscopic surgery, 120
Aspirin, 125
Auckland Marathon, 107